Abolition Movement

Recent Titles in
Landmarks of the American Mosaic

Wounded Knee Massacre
Martin Gitlin

Abolition Movement

T. Adams Upchurch

Landmarks of the American Mosaic

 GREENWOOD

AN IMPRINT OF ABC-CLIO, LLC
Santa Barbara, California • Denver, Colorado • Oxford, England

Library of Congress Cataloging-in-Publication Data

Upchurch, Thomas Adams.
    Abolition movement / T. Adams Upchurch.
        p. cm. — (Landmarks of the American mosaic)
    Includes bibliographical references and index.
    ISBN 978–0–313–38606–0 (hard copy : alk. paper) — ISBN 978–0–313–38607–7
(e-book)
1. Antislavery movements—United States—History. 2. Slavery—United States—
History. 3. Abolitionists—United States—Biography. I. Title.
E441.U6   2011
326′.80973—dc22   2010037170

ISBN: 978–0–313–38606–0
EISBN: 978–0–313–38607–7

15 14 13 12 11   1 2 3 4 5

This book is also available on the World Wide Web as an eBook.
Visit www.abc-clio.com for details.

Greenwood
An Imprint of ABC-CLIO, LLC

ABC-CLIO, LLC
130 Cremona Drive, P.O. Box 1911
Santa Barbara, California 93116-1911

This book is printed on acid-free paper ∞

Manufactured in the United States of America

My sincere thanks go out to Alan Brasher for generously allowing me to peruse his doctoral dissertation on Transcendentalism, to Courtney Joiner for sharing her master's thesis on the Grimke sisters, and to the administration of East Georgia College for providing moral support as I researched, wrote, and published this book.

Contents

Series Foreword

THE LANDMARKS OF THE AMERICAN MOSAIC series comprises individual volumes devoted to exploring an event or development central to this country's multicultural heritage. The topics illuminate the struggles and triumphs of American Indians, African Americans, Latinos, and Asian Americans, from European contact through the turbulent last half of the twentieth century. The series covers landmark court cases, laws, government programs, civil rights infringements, riots, battles, movements, and more. Written by historians especially for high school students, undergraduates, and general readers, these content-rich references satisfy thorough research needs and provide a deeper understanding of material that students might only be exposed to in a short section of a textbook or a superficial explanation online.

Each book on a particular topic is a one-stop reference source. The series format includes

- Introduction
- Chronology
- Narrative chapters that trace the evolution of the event or topic chronologically
- Biographical profiles of key figures
- Selection of crucial primary documents
- Glossary
- Bibliography
- Index

This landmark series promotes respect for cultural diversity and supports the social studies curriculum by helping students understand multicultural American history.

Introduction

RARELY IS IT EASY for scholars to determine the exact moment of creation of a "movement" in history. Movements are generally the result of years of gestation and birth pangs before one defining event announces to the world that something of lasting historical importance is going on. Such is the case with the American abolition or "abolitionist" movement, as it is interchangeably known. From the Colonial Era, when slavery was still a common practice throughout the world, to the Early Republic phase of U.S. history, when it began to evolve into the South's "peculiar institution," there had always been a small minority of Americans who opposed and protested against slavery. These critics of slavery were not organized, however, and therefore did not constitute a movement. Generally, their dislike of slavery resulted from their personal Christian religious views, and they consequently treated slavery as a moral rather than a political issue. This put the focus of their opposition more on slave traders and slave holders than on a government and worked more on the heart and soul of the individual than on a legislative body's collective conscience. This abolition strategy came to be known as "moral suasion."

Even though the Founding Fathers occasionally discussed and debated the politics of slavery, as they did in the Constitutional Convention of 1787, slavery was not seen as a top priority for the young nation's attention, much less the great question of the day that it became to the next generation. Indeed, from the 1780s to the 1810s, the vast majority of Americans believed the nascent United States had more urgent, pressing concerns that must be addressed, such as establishing and stabilizing the new government, determining the powers allotted to each branch, and sorting through constitutional differences that led to the creation of political parties. Then there were national defense, foreign affairs, and military issues, as well as economic growth, domestic commerce, international trade, and financial soundness, just to name some of the most obvious things that screamed for governmental attention. All of these matters had to be addressed first, or so most Americans thought at that time, if the United States was to survive long enough to get the chance to address other problems, the foremost of them being slavery.

Not until after the War of 1812 and the Napoleonic Wars did American political leaders have the luxury of considering the growth of slavery as a top priority, and their solution was not the legal abolition of slavery but rather voluntary manumission and colonization of freed slaves in Africa. The American Colonization Society was founded in 1816 to promote that ideal. Even then, the colonization movement had barely begun when the Missouri Controversy of 1819 to 1820 awakened the nation to the seriousness and immediacy of the politics of the slavery issue. As Thomas Jefferson put it, the question of whether Missouri (the first territory completely west of the Mississippi River to apply for statehood) should become a slave state sounded an alarm "like a fire-bell in the night." Suddenly, Americans realized that on top of the old problem of slavery growing where it already existed, it was also spreading to the great vast expanses of the American West, and that would be the great battleground between antislavery reformers and proslavery apologists in the coming years.

Even with the coming of that "fire-bell in the night," slavery commanded the attention of the nation only briefly, such that the few true, uncompromising abolitionists who were out there, such as Benjamin Lundy—pioneers clearing the way for the coming movement—were largely ignored. The election of the first openly proslavery president of the United States, Andrew Jackson, in 1828, signaled the start of a new epoch in American history in which abolitionists would begin to take center stage, and they would do it with far more radical rhetoric than had ever been used before. It would be so radical, in fact, as to polarize people, forcing them to choose sides in what would be the nation's greatest culture war.

In the year of Jackson's inauguration, 1829, a free black Bostonian named David Walker fired the metaphoric first shot in the culture war when he published his *Appeal to the Colored Citizens of the*

World, urging slaves to rise up in violent rebellion and throw off their chains of bondage. When scholars look for the starting point of the abolition "movement," this is where many find it. But other scholars find it two years later in Boston, when a young white reformer named William Lloyd Garrison began publishing his radical weekly newspaper, the *Liberator*, urging not that slaves take responsibility for making themselves free but that fellow white professing Christians rise up in righteous indignation against slavery. Garrison, unlike most white antislavery reformers before him, did not pull any punches but rather waged a war of words against slavery in no uncertain terms, calling it the most heinous sin against God and crime against humanity that ever the mind of mankind conceived. Whether Walker and the *Appeal* or Garrison and the *Liberator* started the abolition movement is unimportant in the big scheme. The point is that they combined with other equally notable people and events in the early 1830s to ensure that a full-scale crusade to destroy slavery in America occurred. (The most important factors specifically were the Nat Turner slave rebellion in 1831, and the creation of the American Anti-Slavery Society and the abolition of slavery in the British empire in 1833.)

The fact that a movement had begun in the early 1830s did not mean that suddenly a majority of Americans joined it, supported it, or even gave tacit approval to it. Actually, quite the opposite was the case. In the first decade, not more than perhaps 1 percent of Americans would have been even remotely termed "abolitionists" or supporters of abolitionism. If it appears otherwise in retrospect, it is only because the leaders of that 1 percent tended to be highly visible and extremely vocal, garnering attention out of all proportion to their number. Despite all the attention and despite their considerable efforts at evangelical proselytizing, the abolitionists did not have much success at recruiting their fellow Americans to join their cause in the early years. The average American, instead, considered them a bunch of religious radicals who knew little or nothing about the reality of the slaves' plight or of the typical master–slave relationship, and regardless of his personal feelings about slavery, did not want to be associated with that strange little fringe group.

Interestingly, the thing that really did the most to swell the ranks of the abolitionists in the 1830s was persecution. This persecution came at the hands of otherwise mild-mannered neighbors in northern towns and cities, at the hands of radical proslavery southerners and their state governments, and ultimately at the hands of the leaders of the U.S. government. After a spate of such anti-abolitionist activity in 1835 to 1836 and particularly after the murder of Elijah Lovejoy in Illinois in 1837, the number of abolitionists doubled. And yet there was no consistency in growth thereafter. The whole decade of the 1840s was one of taking two steps forward and one step back. Divided by women's rights and various lesser reform issues, confused by the as-yet undefined place of black speakers and writers such as the silver-tongued Frederick Douglass and the inflammatory Henry Highland Garnet in the ranks, and convoluted by the abolitionists' entry into national third-party politics via the Liberty Party and the Free Soil Party, the movement seemed to be wandering in the wilderness with no clear direction. And although these distractions stole most of the attention, the creation of the American Missionary Association (AMA) actually became the most important development of the 1840s in terms of its impact on growing the movement. The AMA was a philanthropic abolitionist organization devoted to ministering to the physical and spiritual needs of free blacks on the fringes of society, mainly in Canada, the Caribbean, and Liberia. It served to help thousands of Americans fulfill their Christian humanitarian impulses, if sometimes merely by allowing them to give money to an exotic, worthy cause.

The early 1850s brought forth events that cleared things up considerably, at least in the sense that they galvanized a large segment of the northern public against slavery. The first was the passage of the new Fugitive Slave Act as part of the Compromise of 1850. It required northern states to aid in the capture and return of runaway slaves, a practice that many northerners found completely reprehensible. It generated the greatest outcry and resistance yet seen against the peculiar institution, and it had the opposite effect of what was intended—it actually caused traffic on the Underground Railroad to increase dramatically. Two years later, a petite white female writer named Harriet Beecher Stowe took the country by storm with her novel *Uncle Tom's Cabin*. As a recruiting tool, it was far more effective than Garrison's *Liberator* newspaper and just as effective, if not more so, than Theodore Dwight Weld's monumental 1837 book *Slavery As It Is*.

The mid-1850s saw a fast-moving chain of events that gave even greater impetus to the abolitionists. The Kansas-Nebraska Act, which led to the "Bleeding Kansas" saga and the concomitant "Bleeding Sumner" affair, gripped the nation's attention from 1854 to 1856, and the U.S. Supreme Court ruling in *Scott v. Sandford* in 1857 and John Brown's raid on Harpers Ferry in 1859 brought the issue of slavery to a fever pitch. Thereafter, it seemed not a matter of whether the Union of free states and slave states would be dissolved but merely how long before the dissolution happened. The election of the first Republican president, Abraham Lincoln, in 1860, ended whatever slim hope remained of saving the Union. South Carolina's secession, followed quickly by the secession of six other southern states and the creation of the Confederate States of America, soon brought the inevitable showdown between the proslavery and antislavery states on that great stage of history known as the Civil War.

The war itself was not exclusively about slavery. On that point, Lincoln, his Confederate counterpart Jefferson Davis, and many historians who have studied it since agree. Yet slavery, or more accurately the national schizophrenia about it, was the great catalyst of events that pushed the country to war. For at the very heart of the American experiment in self-government from its inception in 1776 lay the ideal of freedom and equality for all, and nothing else seemed so incongruous with that goal as human bondage in the form of chattel slavery. It is difficult, if not impossible, therefore, to imagine a scenario in which the Union would have been broken up over any other issue than this one, which polarized Americans into northerners and southerners, progressive democratic egalitarians and conservative property rights constitutionalists, and self-proclaimed "real Christians" and their alleged hypocrite counterparts.

The war invigorated the abolitionists and their cause. Although Lincoln had repeatedly disavowed abolitionism (while simultaneously expressing his antislavery opinions), he could do nothing less in the end than free the slaves. Thus, the long history of slavery in America met its demise on the field of battle not in the 30-year war of words between abolitionists and proslavery apologists but on the actual battlefields of the Civil War. It was nonetheless a victory for the abolitionists all the same. William Lloyd Garrison and many of the original radical reformers lived to see it and to benefit from it in terms of how people have viewed them ever since. Indeed, the abolitionists came out looking like the good guys, the heroes and heroines, so to speak, in what was the greatest and longest running drama in American history.

This book details that story. The narrative begins by whisking through hundreds of years of history and briefly surveying the old-world origins of the African slave trade. It traces slavery's growth in the South from a problem inherited from the English colonial system to the "peculiar institution" that southern leaders came to trumpet as a "positive good" for America. It highlights preliminary efforts to limit the growth of slavery through voluntary manumission, state law, and the colonization movement. It follows the story of the "slavocracy's" attempts to expand the institution to the West, and finally it focuses on the abolitionists' attempts to end it from the 1830s to 1865. The book also contains supplements to the narrative, including a fairly detailed chronology, a wide assortment of primary source documents, a collection of mini biographies of the main figures in the movement, a glossary of terms associated with the movement, and an annotated bibliography of some of the major books written on the topic over the past century and a half. The author makes no pretense of adding much original information to what is already widely available, but he hopes the way the material is presented here will offer a fresh perspective and a few enlightening insights for students and lay readers.

Chronology of American Slavery and Abolitionism

1619 The first African slaves are brought to Jamestown, Virginia, an English colony.

1661 Virginia recognizes slavery by law as something distinct from indentured servitude.

1662 Virginia codifies hereditary slavery based on the status of the mother.

1672 The Royal African Company is created, increasing the amount of slave trading to the English colonies of the future United States.

1686 South Carolina becomes the first future U.S. state to pass Slave Codes, putting slaves under a different set of laws and societal rules than free people live under.

1688 Quakers in Pennsylvania issue the "Germantown Protest," the first public antislavery statement in American history.

1700 Samuel Sewall publishes *The Selling of Joseph*, the first anti-slavery publication in America.

1705 Virginia codifies slaves as property, allowing owners to execute runaways and transfer ownership to others upon their death.

1711 The Pennsylvania colonial assembly votes to outlaw slavery, but the British government overrules the decision.

1712 The first major slave revolt in an English colony in the future United States occurs in New York City.

1729   Benjamin Franklin publishes Ralph Sandiford's Quaker anti-slavery tract *A Brief Examination of the Practice of the Times* in Philadelphia.

1732   Georgia becomes the first English colony in the future United States to prohibit slavery in its charter.

1737   Benjamin Lay, a Pennsylvania Quaker, publishes *All Slave-Keepers, That Keep the Innocent in Bondage.*

1739   The Stono Rebellion slave uprising occurs in South Carolina.

1741   The hanging of slaves and free conspirators begins, lasting more than two months, after a series of arsons in New York City.

1749   Georgia rescinds its prohibition against slavery.

1753   Quaker preacher John Woolman publishes the first volume of *Some Considerations on the Keeping of Negroes.*

1754   Quaker preachers Anthony Benezet and John Woolman publish the antislavery tract *An Epistle of Caution and Advice.*

1758   The Pennsylvania Annual Meeting of Quakers makes its first official statement denouncing slavery.

1759   Anthony Benezet publishes his *Observations on the Inslaving, Importing and Purchasing of Negroes.*

1762   Benjamin Franklin publishes John Woolman's *Part Second* of *Some Considerations on the Keeping of Negroes.*

1766   Benezet publishes *A Caution and Warning to Great Britain and Her Colonies on the Calamitous State of the Enslaved Negroes.*

1773   William Dillwyn publishes *Brief Considerations on Slavery* in Philadelphia.

Poetry of the black woman Phyllis Wheatley is published in London.

1775   Pennsylvania Quakers organize the Society for the Relief of Free Negroes Unlawfully Held in Bondage, the first antislavery society in American history.

Benjamin Rush publishes *An Address to the Inhabitants of the British Colonies in America, Upon Slave-keeping.*

Thomas Paine publishes an antislavery article in the *Pennsylvania Journal* called "African Slavery in America" and publishes a pamphlet called *A Serious Thought* that rails against slavery.

Governor of Virginia, Lord Dunmore, promises slaves freedom if they become Loyalists.

Continental Congress's ban on importation of foreign slaves takes effect.

George Washington and the Continental Army begin enlisting black soldiers for the Revolution.

Connecticut clergyman Levi Hart proposes the first compensated emancipation plan.

1776   The Continental Congress suspends the slave trade.

Samuel Hopkins, a New England Congregationalist, publishes *A Dialogue Concerning the Slavery of the Africans.*

1777   Slaves in Massachusetts petition the state government for emancipation.

Vermont becomes the first future U.S. state to outlaw slavery.

1780   Pennsylvania passes the first gradual emancipation law.

1783   The Massachusetts Supreme Court declares slavery unconstitutional in *Commonwealth v. Jennison.*

1784   Connecticut passes a gradual emancipation law.

The Continental Congress outlaws slavery in the Northwest Territories.

Virginia frees slaves who fought for the American side in the Revolution.

1785   The New York Society for Promoting the Manumission of Slaves is founded, with John Jay as president.

1787   The U.S. Constitution requires a ban on the importation of foreign-born slaves within 20 years and counts 60 percent of the slave population for congressional apportionment.

Isaac Hopper, a Philadelphia Quaker, begins what will later become known as the Underground Railroad.

1789   Delaware outlaws the slave trade.

The Maryland Abolition Society is founded.

1790   The Pennsylvania Society for Promoting the Abolition of Slavery petitions the U.S. government to end slavery.

Massachusetts congressman Elbridge Gerry proposes a compensated emancipation plan using money from the sale of federal land to purchase slaves.

1791   Zephaniah Swift delivers *An Oration on American Slavery* at the Connecticut Society for the Promotion of Freedom, and the Relief of Persons unlawfully holden in Bondage, while Jonathan Edwards delivers *Injustice and Impolicy of the Slave Trade, and of the Slavery of Africans* at another meeting of the same organization.

1792   David Rice delivers the speech *Slavery Inconsistent with Justice and Good Policy* at a Danville, Kentucky, antislavery meeting; the speech is published in Philadelphia.

1793   Noah Webster publishes *Effects of Slavery on Morals and Industry.*

The U.S. government passes the first Fugitive Slave Law, making it illegal to aid runaway slaves and allowing owners to cross state lines to catch fugitives.

Eli Whitney is awarded a patent for his cotton gin.

Georgia outlaws the importation of foreign-born slaves.

1794   The U.S. government outlaws Americans engaging in slave trade in non-U.S. ports and outlaws American ports outfitting foreign slave trading ships.

1796   The American Convention for Promoting the Abolition of Slavery, and Improving the Condition of the African Race holds its third national convention in Philadelphia; delegates from seven different local abolition societies attend: New York, New Jersey, Pennsylvania, Maryland, Virginia, Providence (Rhode Island), and Wilmington (Delaware).

1797   The American Convention for Promoting the Abolition of Slavery, and Improving the Condition of the African Race holds its fourth national convention in Philadelphia; delegates attend from local societies in New York, New Jersey, Pennsylvania, Baltimore

(Maryland), Alexandria (Virginia), Richmond (Virginia), and Choptank (Delaware).

1798 The American Convention for Promoting the Abolition of Slavery, and Improving the Condition of the African Race holds its fifth national convention in Philadelphia; only four local chapters send delegates.

1799 New York passes a gradual emancipation law.

1800 Gabriel Prosser is hanged in Virginia for plotting a slave rebellion.

Future abolitionist John Brown is born in Torrington, Connecticut.

1803 South Carolina openly violates the U.S. government's 1794 ban on outfitting foreign slave ships.

1804 The new state of Ohio becomes first in the United States to pass Black Codes, designed to discourage fugitive slaves from seeking refuge there.

1805 Future abolitionist William Lloyd Garrison is born in Newburyport, Massachusetts.

1807 The U.S. government passes the constitutionally required law banning the importation of foreign-born slaves.

1808 The U.S. government's ban on importation of foreign-born slaves takes effect.

1809 Abraham Lincoln is born in Kentucky.

1815 Paul Cuffe, a free black man from Connecticut, takes 35 of his fellow blacks to be colonized in the African nation of Sierra Leone.

Roberts Vaux publishes *Memoirs of the Lives of Benjamin Lay and Ralph Sandiford*, one of the first books to memorialize pioneers of the abolition movement.

1816 The American Colonization Society is formed in Washington, D.C.

1817 Charles Osborn publishes the *Philanthropist*, the first known antislavery newspaper in American history, in Mount Pleasant, Ohio.

Roberts Vaux publishes *Memoirs of the Life of Anthony Benezet.*

1819   Elihu Embree publishes the *Manumission Intelligencer* in Jonesborough, Tennessee, the first newspaper devoted exclusively to abolition in American history; the newspaper is known as the *Emancipator* by 1820.

Former U.S. President James Madison endorses a compensated emancipation plan to be financed through the sale of federal land.

The Missouri Controversy becomes the first major episode in American history in which the spread of slavery is a polarizing political issue.

1820   The Missouri Compromise settles the first major dispute between the North and the South over slavery.

The slave-carrying pirate ship *Antelope* is captured by U.S. government officials.

The American Colonization Society sends its first 88 colonists to be settled in what would soon become Liberia.

1821   Benjamin Lundy, in Mount Pleasant, Ohio, begins publishing the *Genius of Universal Emancipation.*

Fanny Wright of Scotland publishes *Views of Society and Manners in America.*

Liberia is created by agreement between the American Colonization Society, the government of Great Britain, and local African tribes.

1822   Denmark Vesey and his fellow slave uprising conspirators are hanged in South Carolina.

1823   John Rankin writes a series of essays soon to become his book *Letters on Slavery* in Ohio.

1824   English abolitionist Elizabeth Heyrick publishes her *Immediate, Not Gradual Abolition;* Lundy soon reprints it serially in the *Genius of Universal Emancipation.*

1825   The U.S. Supreme Court rules on complex international issues in the *Antelope* case, compensating Spanish and Portuguese slave holders for stolen property while liberating 120 slaves and sending them to Liberia.

The American Tract Society is founded.

Fanny Wright publishes *A Plan for the Gradual Abolition of Slavery in the United States Without Danger of Loss to the Citizens of the South*.

1827 Mexico prohibits slavery in Texas.

1828 Garrison's reform paper, *Journal of the Times*, is first published in Bennington, Vermont.

Benjamin Lundy founds the National Anti-Slavery Tract Society in Baltimore.

1829 Garrison delivers an antislavery address to the Congregational Society in Boston, making his name known in Boston for the first time.

Garrison begins writing for Lundy's *Genius of Universal Emancipation*.

David Walker's *Appeal to the Colored Citizens of the World* is published.

Philadelphia female abolitionists organize the first boycott against southern cotton, which was the forerunner of the Free Produce Movement.

1830 Garrison begins a 49-day sentence in Baltimore jail for libel in the case of *The State of Maryland v. The Genius of Universal Emancipation*.

Garrison begins a series of antislavery speeches in Boston, making many converts to abolitionism.

1831 Garrison publishes the first edition of the *Liberator*.

In Virginia, Nat Turner stages the deadliest slave rebellion in American history.

Bostonians begin the process of creating the New England Anti-Slavery Society.

1832 The New England Anti-Slavery Society is formed.

The Salem Female Anti-Slavery Society is formed in Massachusetts.

The Rhode Island Anti-Slavery Society is formed.

Elizur Wright publishes *The Sin of Slavery, and Its Remedy; Containing Some Reflections on the Moral Influences of African Colonization.*

Garrison publishes his *Thoughts on Colonization.*

1833   Prudence Crandall begins admitting black girls to the Female Boarding School in Canterbury, Connecticut.

The first World Antislavery Convention is held in London.

Connecticut passes the Black Law, designed to stop Crandall's practice of admitting black students.

Crandall is jailed and tried for violating the Black Law.

The New York Anti-Slavery Society holds its first meeting.

The Maine Anti-Slavery Society is formed.

Oberlin College, the first institution of higher education in the United States founded by abolitionists for training students to become abolitionists, is founded in Ohio.

Lydia Maria Child publishes *An Appeal in Favor of that Class of Americans Called Africans.*

David Lee Child publishes *The Despotism of Freedom.*

John Greenleaf Whittier publishes his first antislavery book, *Justice and Expediency.*

The American Anti-Slavery Society is formed in Philadelphia.

Lucretia Mott founds the Philadelphia Female Anti-Slavery Society.

1834   Amos Phelps publishes *Lectures on Slavery and Its Remedy.*

Students at Lane Seminary in Cincinnati begin 18 days of debates on immediate versus gradual emancipation of slaves.

Lewis Tappan's New York home is vandalized by a proslavery mob intent upon terrorizing the abolitionist.

Crandall's Female Boarding School in Connecticut closes.

Orson S. Murray buys the *Vermont Telegraph* and turns it into a radical abolitionist paper.

1835   The American Union for the Relief and Improvement of the Colored Race is formed in Boston.

The Boston Female Anti-Slavery Society is formed.

The Kentucky Anti-Slavery Society is formed.

Amos Dresser is publicly whipped for his abolitionist activities in Nashville, Tennessee.

The American Anti-Slavery Society initiates its Great Postal Campaign for sending abolitionist literature to the South via the U.S. mail.

The U.S. Post Office in Charleston, South Carolina, is raided by a proslavery mob seeking to confiscate abolitionist literature; the city's postmaster thereafter stops delivery of antislavery materials.

U.S. President Andrew Jackson urges Congress to pass a law stopping the shipment of abolitionist literature to southern states.

The city of Boston holds a public meeting and denounces the abolition movement.

Garrison is jailed in Boston to protect him from a lynch mob.

Unitarian and Transcendentalist preacher William Ellery Channing of Boston publishes his antislavery book *Negro Slavery*.

Lydia Maria Child publishes *Authentic Anecdotes of American Slavery*.

French writer Gustave Auguste de Beaumont publishes *Marie, or Slavery in the United States*.

French writer Alexis de Tocqueville's *Democracy in America* denounces slavery.

Elizur Wright publishes *On Abstinence from Products of Slave Labor*.

1836   Angelina Grimke publishes *An Appeal to the Christian Women of the South*.

Sarah Grimke publishes *An Epistle to the Clergy of the Southern States*.

Lydia Maria Child publishes *Evils of Slavery and the Cure of Slavery* and the *Anti-Slavery Catechism*.

The New England Antislavery Society changes its name to the Massachusetts Antislavery Society.

The Grimke sisters begin speaking on the American Antislavery Society's Circuit, mixing the women's rights question with abolitionism.

James G. Birney founds *The Philanthropist* newspaper in Ohio; his office in Cincinnati is attacked by a proslavery mob.

Benjamin Lundy founds the *National Enquirer* in Philadelphia.

Charles Ball publishes his *The Life and Adventures of a Fugitive Slave* anonymously; the following year, it is reprinted as *Slavery in the United States: A Narrative of the Life and Adventures of Charles Ball.*

The U.S. House of Representatives passes the Gag Rule, preventing abolitionist congressmen from presenting antislavery petitions.

Texas wins its independence from Mexico and applies for admission to the U.S. Congress as a slave state.

The Massachusetts Supreme Court rules in *Commonwealth v. Aves* that slaves brought into the state are automatically free under Massachusetts law.

Samuel May, Unitarian minister and abolitionist, is attacked by a proslavery mob in Montpelier, Vermont.

A Narrative of the Adventures and Escape of Moses Roper, From American Slavery is published in England; it is published in the United States in 1837.

1837   Angelina Grimke publishes *An Appeal to the Women of the Nominally Free States.*

English writer Harriet Martineau's *Society in America* denounces slavery.

Abraham Lincoln and other members of the Illinois legislature publicly denounce the abolition movement.

Thaddeus Stevens of Pennsylvania converts to become an abolitionist.

Boston abolitionists answer charges of the State of Massachusetts's Lunt Committee.

Members of the General Association of Congregational Ministers publish "The Appeal of the Clerical Abolitionists on Antislavery Measures," denouncing Garrisonianism.

Abolitionist Elijah Lovejoy is murdered in Alton, Illinois, and his press is destroyed.

1838   Theodore Dwight Weld, leader of the Lane Rebels, and Angelina Grimke get married.

Pennsylvania Hall in Philadelphia, meeting site of Anti-Slavery Convention of American Women, is burned by a proslavery mob.

John Greenleaf Whittier takes over the *National Enquirer* and renames it the *Pennsylvania Freeman.*

Whittier publishes his first collection of abolitionist poetry, simply entitled *Poems.*

Runaway slave Frederick Bailey of Maryland reaches the North and changes his name to Frederick Douglass.

Joshua Giddings of Ohio becomes the first self-described abolitionist to be elected to Congress.

The Female Vigilant Committee is formed by blacks in Philadelphia to support the Underground Railroad.

1839   The British Navy charges two American ships with slave trading.

The slave ship *Amistad* experiences a mutiny and arrives at port in Connecticut.

Benjamin Lundy dies in Illinois.

Maria Weston Chapman of the Boston Female Anti-Slavery Society begins publication of the annual compilation of abolitionist writings called *The Liberty Bell.*

1840   The great abolitionist schism occurs at the American Anti-Slavery Society convention in New York, soon leading to the founding of the American and Foreign Antislavery Society.

The American and Foreign Anti-Slavery Society continues publishing the *Emancipator* as its official voice in print.

The American Anti-Slavery Society begins publishing the *National Anti-Slavery Standard* as its official voice in print.

The Liberty Party holds a national convention in Albany, New York, and nominates James G. Birney for U.S. president; Birney receives only 7,000 votes in the presidential election.

Birney's *The American Churches: The Bulwarks of American Slavery* is published in England; it is not published in the United States until 1842.

Theodore Sedgwick Wright and Samuel Cornish publish the anticolonization book *The Colonization Scheme Considered.*

Cyrus P. Grosvenor publishes *Slavery vs. the Bible.*

The U.S. Supreme Court begins hearing the *Amistad* case.

The slave-carrying ship *Hermosa* wrecks in the Bahamas; British authorities liberate the American slaves, setting off an international claims dispute.

Massachusetts congressman and former U.S. President John Quincy Adams, in defiance of the Gag Rule, presents more than 500 antislavery petitions to the House of Representatives.

The American Anti-Slavery Society compiles *Slavery and the Internal Slave Trade in the United States* for the World Anti-Slavery Convention in London.

The World Anti-Slavery Convention meets and refuses to welcome American female delegates.

1841   The Portland Anti-Slavery Society is formed in Maine.

The U.S. Supreme Court rules in favor of the Africans in the *Amistad* case, resulting in 35 Africans returning home.

Slaves seize control of the ship *Creole* and flee to freedom in the British Bahamas.

William Lloyd Garrison meets Frederick Douglass for the first time at an antislavery convention in Massachusetts.

Thornton Stringfellow publishes the proslavery book *A Brief Examination of Scripture Testimony on the Institution of Slavery.*

1842 The U.S. Supreme Court rules in *Prigg v. Pennsylvania* that free states are not required to catch or return fugitive slaves.

The Lattimer Committee is formed in Massachusetts to defend fugitive slaves against slave catchers; it sends an antislavery petition with more than 50,000 signatures to Congress.

In the Webster-Ashburton Treaty, the United States and Great Britain agree to cooperate to stop slave trafficking.

William Ellery Channing publishes *The Duty of the Free States*, arguing for civil disobedience against proslavery federal laws.

Charles Turner Torrey allegedly coins the term "Underground Railroad."

1843 Isabella Baumfree Van Wagener changes her name to Sojourner Truth, and begins her career as the most famous black female abolitionist public speaker.

Stephen S. Foster publishes *The Brotherhood of Thieves, or, a True Picture of the American Church and Clergy*, which scolds preachers in the North and South for hypocrisy on the slavery issue.

Moses Grandy publishes his *Narrative of the Life of Moses Grandy; Late Slave in the United States of America*.

The Second World Anti-Slavery Convention meets in London.

1844 The U.S. House of Representatives rescinds the Gag Rule.

James G. Birney of the Liberty Party receives 62,000 votes in the presidential election.

The Methodist Church in America splits over the slavery issue.

Charles Tuner Torrey is convicted in Maryland of helping slaves escape and sentenced to six years in prison.

1845 Texas, over objections from antislavery people, is admitted to the Union as a slave state.

The Baptist Church in America splits over the slavery issue.

Abby Kelley Foster founds the *Anti-Slavery Bugle* in Salem, Ohio.

Cassius M. Clay publishes his antislavery paper the *True American* in Lexington, Kentucky, before relocating it in Cincinnati, Ohio.

Lysander Spooner publishes *The Unconstitutionality of Slavery.*

William Goodell publishes *Come Outer-ism, the Duty of Secession from a Corrupt Church.*

1846   James G. Birney moves to Washington, D.C., and renames his *Philanthropist* newspaper the *National Era.*

The American Missionary Association is formed and soon becomes the largest abolitionist organization in the United States.

Garrison helps found a new Antislavery League in England.

Mexico and the United States declare war.

Congressman David Wilmot of Pennsylvania proposes that the United States make any territory acquired in the Mexican War free from slavery.

J. C. Lovejoy publishes the story of two escaped slaves from Kentucky called *Interesting Memoirs and Documents Relating to American Slavery and the Glorious Struggle Now Making for Complete Emancipation* in England; it is reprinted in the United States as *Narratives of the Sufferings of Lewis and Milton Clarke.*

John Greenleaf Whittier publishes his most famous collection of abolitionist poems, *Voices of Freedom.*

1847   Dred Scott, a slave in St. Louis, files a legal suit for his freedom in Missouri.

Jones v. Van Zandt upholds the Fugitive Slave Act of 1793.

John Brown meets Frederick Douglass for the first time.

William Wells Brown publishes his *Narrative of William W. Brown, A Fugitive Slave.*

Cyrus P. Grosvenor publishes *A Review of the "Correspondence" of Messrs. Fuller and Wayland on the Subject of American Slavery.*

Henry Ward Beecher begins pastoring the Plymouth Congregational Church in Brooklyn, New York, which becomes the self-described "Grand Central Depot" of the Underground Railroad.

Parker Pillsbury publishes *The Church As It Is; or The Forlorn Hope of Slavery.*

1848 The United States wins the Mexican War and acquires the Mexican Cession lands, adding another third to the geographic size of the nation.

John Brown moves to Gerrit Smith's Timbuktoo community in New York and begins mentoring free blacks.

The Free Soil Party is formed; it nominates former Democrat Martin Van Buren for U.S. president; Van Buren garners more than 200,000 votes.

1849 Southern states meet in the Nashville Convention to discuss secession if the Mexican Cession territory of California is made a free state.

Henry Bibb publishes his *Narrative of the Life and Adventures of Henry Bibb, an American Slave; Written by Himself.*

Josiah Henson publishes *The Life of Josiah Henson.*

Harriet Tubman escapes from slavery in Maryland via the Underground Railroad.

1850 Garrison publishes *The Narrative of Sojourner Truth: A Northern Slave.*

The Fugitive Slave; or, Events in the History of James W. C. Pennington is published.

Lysander Spooner publishes *A Defense for Fugitive Slaves.*

The U.S. government passes the second Fugitive Slave Act, abolishes slave auctions in Washington, D.C., and gives each Mexican Cession territory except for California popular sovereignty, all as parts of the Compromise of 1850.

1851 The *National Era* abolitionist newspaper begins serial publication of Harriet Beecher Stowe's *Uncle Tom's Cabin.*

Henry Brown publishes his *Narrative of the Life of Henry Box Brown, Written by Himself* about his escape from slavery.

John G. Fee of Kentucky publishes *An Anti-Slavery Manual, or the Wrongs of American Slavery Exposed by the Light of the Bible.*

Blacks in Christiana, Pennsylvania, resist a Fugitive Slave Act posse.

Abolitionists break into a Syracuse, New York, jail to liberate fugitive slave Jerry McHenry.

The Shadrach Minkins fugitive slave case in Boston stirs national attention.

John Brown organizes the League of Gileadites in Springfield, Massachusetts, to defend fugitive slaves from slave catchers.

1852   Harriet Beecher Stowe's novel *Uncle Tom's Cabin* is published in book form.

Joshua Glover escapes from slavery in St. Louis, settling in Wisconsin; his capture two years later by federal officers leads to the major case over the Fugitive Slave Act of 1850, *Ableman v. Booth.*

1853   Harriet Beecher Stowe publishes *The Making of Uncle Tom's Cabin.*

Lydia Maria Child publishes *Isaac T. Hopper: A True Life.*

Solomon Northup publishes *Twelve Years a Slave.*

1854   The Kansas-Nebraska Act is passed, opening Kansas to a popular sovereignty referendum on slavery.

The New England Emigrant Aid Society is formed to support settlement of abolitionists in Kansas.

Three of John Brown's sons move to Kansas and set up an abolitionist camp called Brown's Station.

The New York-Kansas League is formed.

George Fitzhugh publishes his proslavery book, *Sociology for the South.*

The American and Foreign Anti-Slavery Society publishes the *Personal Memoir of Daniel Drayton.*

The *Pennsylvania Freeman* and the *National Anti-Slavery Standard* merge.

Samuel Hopkins's *Timely Articles on Slavery* is published posthumously.

Garrison publicly burns the U.S. Constitution in Framingham, Massachusetts.

The Republican Party is organized in Ripon, Wisconsin.

The Ashmun Institute (today Lincoln University), the first black liberal arts college in America, is founded by Presbyterians in Pennsylvania.

The racially integrated Berea College in Kentucky is founded.

An international commission negotiates settlements in the *Creole, Hermosa,* and *Enterprize* claims cases.

The fugitive slave Anthony Burns is forcibly removed from Boston to Virginia by federal troops amid great disapproval from abolitionists.

1855   John Brown goes to Kansas and leads a group of abolitionists in defending the town of Lawrence against attack by a proslavery force.

The Know-Nothing Party splits over the slavery issue.

Great Britain pays the United States $110,000 in reparations over the *Creole* case of 1841.

Maria Weston Chapman publishes *How Can I Help Abolish Slavery?*

Eliza Follen publishes *Anti-Slavery Hymns and Songs* and *A Letter to Mothers in Free States.*

Samuel Ringgold Ward publishes his *Autobiography of a Fugitive Slave.*

Peter Randolph publishes *Sketches of Slave Life; or, Illustrations of the "Peculiar Institution."*

1856   Lawrence, Kansas, falls to the proslavery force.

George Fitzhugh publishes his pro-slavery book, *Cannibals All!*

Charles Sumner of Massachusetts delivers his Bleeding Kansas speech in the U.S. Senate.

Congressman Preston Brooks of South Carolina canes Sumner in the U.S. Senate.

John Brown and his group commit the Pottawatomie Creek Massacre.

The Republican Party holds its first national convention in Philadelphia, nominating John C. Fremont for U.S. president.

The Margaret Garner fugitive slave and murder case in Cincinnati captures the nation's attention.

Horace Greeley publishes his *History of the Struggle for Slavery Extension or Restriction in the United States.*

1857   The Presbyterian Church begins rupturing over slavery.

The U.S. Supreme courts issues its ruling in the Dred Scott case.

John Brown meets with the Secret Six and tours New England recruiting and raising money for his slave rebellion plan.

Hinton Rowan Helper publishes *The Impending Crisis of the South: How to Meet It.*

Austin Steward publishes his memoir, *Twenty-Two Years a Slave and Forty Years a Free Man.*

1858   John Brown holds an abolitionist convention in Chatham, Ontario, Canada, and then travels to Missouri, where he kills a man and leads 11 slaves toward Canada.

Abraham Lincoln debates U.S. Senator Stephen A. Douglas of Illinois, drawing national attention to his skills as a debater on the slavery issue.

The proslavery Lecompton Constitution is endorsed by U.S. President James Buchanan, but both Congress and the people of Kansas reject it.

1859   The U.S. Supreme Court rules in *Ableman v. Booth* that the Fugitive Slave Act is constitutional.

The American Tract Society splits over the slavery issue.

John Brown begins his raid on the Harpers Ferry, Virginia, arsenal.

John Brown is hanged in Charles Town for attempting to start a slave rebellion in Virginia.

Francis Fredric publishes *The Life and Sufferings of Francis Fredric While in Slavery.*

1860   In November, Abraham Lincoln is nominated by the Republican Party and wins the presidential election.

In December, South Carolina secedes from the Union.

Elizur Wright publishes *An Eye-Opener for the Wide-Awakes.*

1861   Ten more southern states secede from the Union.

Kansas is admitted to the Union as a free state.

In March, Lincoln is sworn in as U.S. president.

In April, Confederate forces fire on U.S. Fort Sumter in Charleston, South Carolina, starting the Civil War.

The U.S. government passes resolution telling Union military officers that it was not their job to enforce the Fugitive Slave Act.

The U.S. government passes the Confiscation Act, permanently freeing slaves liberated by Union forces.

The U.S. Navy begins accepting black sailors into the ranks.

Osborne Perry Anderson publishes *A Voice from Harpers Ferry*, giving a first-hand account of the incidents of the John Brown raid.

David Lee Child publishes the *Rights and Duties of the United States Relative to Slavery Under the Laws of War*.

Lydia Maria Child edits Harriet Jacobs's *Incidents in the Life of a Slave Girl*.

The Presbyterian Church in America officially splits over the slavery issue.

Lincoln endorses a plan for compensated emancipation in Delaware; the Delaware legislature does not take action on it.

1862   Lincoln endorses a plan for compensated emancipation in all border states; Congress supports it, but border state officials reject it.

The U.S. government passes a compensated emancipation law for Washington, D.C., paying slaveholders $300 per slave.

The U.S. government passes a law abolishing slavery in all U.S. territories.

The U.S. government passes a law freeing all slaves who escape to Union states.

Indiana abolitionist and social Utopian Robert Owen urges Lincoln to free the slaves; his letters to Lincoln will soon be published as *The Policy of Emancipation* (1863).

Lincoln announces the Emancipation Proclamation.

Fanny Kemble publishes her *Journal of a Residence on a Georgia Plantation*.

Julia Ward Howe's poem "The Battle Hymn of the Republic" is published in the *Atlantic Monthly*.

Elizur Wright publishes *The Programme of Peace, by a Democrat of the Old South*.

1863   The Emancipation Proclamation takes effect.

The 13th Amendment is proposed in Congress by Owen Lovejoy of Illinois.

The 54th Massachusetts regiment begins recruiting black soldiers.

The battle of Gettysburg comes to a close as Robert E. Lee's Confederate army retreats.

Frederick Douglass meets Abraham Lincoln in Washington, D.C.

1864   Louisiana outlaws slavery within its borders.

Sojourner Truth meets Abraham Lincoln.

Lincoln wins a second term as U.S. president.

1865   Missouri outlaws slavery within its borders.

The Confederate capital of Richmond, Virginia, is sacked by Union troops.

Abraham Lincoln is assassinated in Washington, D.C.

Lincoln's assassin, John Wilkes Booth, is killed in Virginia.

The State of Texas announces the abolition of slavery within its borders.

In December, the 13th Amendment is ratified; slavery is officially abolished.

In December, William Lloyd Garrison ceases publication of the *Liberator*, symbolically ending the 35-year abolition movement.

ONE

From Common Practice to Peculiar Institution: Slavery and Abolitionism to 1816

Slavery's Ancient World Origins and Its New World Evolution

To understand the abolition movement, it is necessary to begin with a brief discussion of slavery. When people think of slavery today, they generally think of the version of it that might best be described as race-based chattel slavery, meaning permanent ownership and complete control of members of the black race by those of the white race. Most of the other mental images of slavery derive from that version of it. Indeed, more often than not, they come from stereotypes about life on the cotton plantations of the deep South from the 1830s to the 1860s: backbreaking work from sunup to sundown; scanty provisions of food, clothes, and housing; regular beatings, rapes, and assorted punishments; the splitting up of families, the selling of children away from their mothers, and miscellaneous other human rights violations. Although these characteristics of slavery have some historical basis in fact, there was far more variety in the institution of slavery than that.

Slavery took many forms over time, and it had different attributes in different geographic areas. For example, most slaves in America before the 1830s lived in towns and cities, not on farms or plantations, and most served as artisans and craftsmen rather than field hands. Slavery cannot accurately be reduced to a single stereotype. The harsh, oppressive, and evil version of slavery described above was ultimately responsible for creating and sustaining the abolition movement in America.

At the heart of the modern stereotype of slavery lies racism. Contrary to popular misconception, the belief that the white race was naturally superior and that the black race was therefore automatically inferior did not exist at the beginning of the African slave trade but rather evolved over a matter of centuries. The role that race and skin color played in American slavery ultimately made it different from earlier forms of slavery and from forms practiced in other places at the same time. When it was fully evolved, the belief in white supremacy was responsible for the worst atrocities associated with slavery, culminating with the degradation of the legal status of blacks to essentially that of livestock in the Dred Scott ruling of the U.S. Supreme Court in 1857. To see how this evolution occurred, the history of slavery must be briefly traced from its origins outside the United States.

Going back to ancient history, most cases of slavery had been caused by one of two things—debt or war. Creditors sometimes collected unpaid debts by taking a proverbial pound of flesh; if there were no more possessions to seize, they took the man who owed them the money, or a member of his family, as payment. In some cases, fathers resorted to selling their children to satisfy their unpaid financial obligations. These cases of slavery generally involved people from the same race, tribe, or nationality, and they created extreme caste structures in those societies in which the rich got richer and the poorest of the poor became slaves. War, however, typically introduced foreign slavery into a culture. Victors took their defeated foes captive, sometimes dragging them hundreds of miles away to the conquering tribe, nation, or empire's homeland. Often, these wars were purely territorial in nature, and the aggressor enjoyed aggrandizement at the expense of neighbors.

Occasionally, religion played the central role in causing slavery, as one group of people believed it was acting upon the dictates of, or with the blessing of, its god or gods in subduing another group, often in a foreign land. This cause of slavery became especially pronounced in Western civilization with the coming of the new religion of Islam in Arabia in the 600s CE. A fundamental tenet of Islam was the belief in Jihad, or holy war, with the idea being that it was Allah's will for all people to be converted, one way or another, whether peacefully through preaching or violently through war.

Islam thus wed two potent causes of slavery, war and religion, into one belief system, making it a juggernaut of change. This belief led to the rapid spread of Islam throughout the Middle East, North Africa, and even into parts of Europe where Christianity previously had been the dominant religion. Indeed, were it not for a couple of decisive victories by Christian armies (most notably at the Battle of Tours in France in the 700s CE), it is possible that all of Europe would have been swallowed up by Islam.

One Christian region of Europe that was indeed overrun and conquered by Muslims was Iberia, the westernmost peninsula of the continent, which is separated from Africa by three miles of water at the Strait of Gibraltar, where modern Portugal and Spain would soon be created. Thereafter, a group of Muslims called Moors from North Africa where Morocco is located today controlled most provinces of Iberia for several centuries. During this time (which historians call the Middle Ages), Muslims took slaves of whatever nations and tribes they conquered, including white Europeans, and sold them to willing buyers throughout the Mediterranean world and beyond. The European Christian Crusades of the High Middle Ages (mainly the 1100s CE), were all about driving Muslims out of territory they held, which Christians believed was rightly theirs. The Europeans encountered great difficulties in these Crusades, finding their dark-skinned foes to be their equals in war-making skills. One result of this hard-fighting was that Crusaders could not consider their whiteness an automatic sign of superiority—far from it, in fact, which is one reason racism was slow in arriving on the slavery scene in history. In cases when the Crusaders succeeded, they reversed the roles of captors and slaves. This reversal had major consequences in Iberia and ultimately in the history of Western civilization as a whole because white Europeans now had opportunity to enslave dark-skinned Moors and their North African neighbors.

The specific Crusade in which the Christians drove the Muslims from power in Iberia was known in Spanish as the *Reconquista*, the reconquest or retaking of land. It was neither a brief nor an easy war to win. Instead, it lasted for hundreds of years and was not declared officially over and won until King Ferdinand and Queen Isabella got married in 1486 and united their provinces of Castile and Aragon into the new, modern nation of Spain. By the time they agreed to sponsor Christopher Columbus's overseas voyage in 1492, North Africa's western coast was being victimized by Portuguese explorers regularly and by Spanish explorers increasingly. Therefore, not surprisingly, African slaves were present on Columbus's voyages to the New World, as well as being on board the other colonists' and explorers' ships that soon followed from Spain and Portugal.

The fact that European masters and African slaves came to the Americas together had huge ramifications not only for American history but for all of world history from then on. For one thing, it meant that as Europeans began colonizing and experimenting with plantation agriculture, they had a labor force readily at hand on the west coast of Africa in case they chose to exploit it. In time, through trial and error, as they sought the best possible labor force for the harsh conditions of their overseas frontiers, they would indeed choose to exploit the Africans. However, not until they had decided that the New World natives, whose proclivity for catching European diseases that killed them or at least made them sick and weak, did not constitute a suitable labor force did they turn their full attention to Africans.

Although there was an obvious racial difference between Europeans and Africans, there was little thought given to race as an automatic determinant of one group's status as masters and the others as slaves. Instead, military power, technological superiority, and religion were the determining factors. As time went on, however, and the Portuguese explorers began moving ever farther down the coast of Africa toward and beyond the equator, seeking a passage to India and the Orient, they encountered non-Muslim, sub-Saharan tribes with darker and darker skin. These groups lived in tribal societies with a wide array of pagan religions, superstitions, and local customs, and their complexions ranged from deep brown to sable black. In the view of Europeans, they were primitive; uneducated; and compared with Muslims, easy to conquer or manipulate.

Even so, differences in the various tribes' size, strength, and business savvy led the Portuguese to make trade relationships with some rather than others. The Yoruba people of the land of Benin were the first to agree to sell their fellow Africans in exchange for exotic European goods. Because the white traders could manipulate one group of blacks to sell them other blacks, those victims of these sales seemed to the whites to be truly at the bottom of the human social hierarchy—inferior to other Africans and thus clearly inferior to themselves. Starting from this seemingly practical rationale, over time, it came to be inferred that blacks were automatically inferior, and to some extent, the darker the complexion, the more inferior the tribe; and likewise, the farther south from Europe, the more inferior the tribe. Add to that the important fact that, to them, the white man's religion of Christianity was the only right and true religion, and there was a perfect concoction of rationales for treating these equatorial and tropical Africans as something less than fully human. (In 1452, Pope Nicholas V actually instructed the leaders of Portugal to enslave pagans in Africa.) Thus their capture, sale, bondage, and removal were rationalized.

Meanwhile, in the early 1500s, both Spain and Portugal grew increasingly involved in establishing transatlantic colonies and in discovering ways to profit from them. After hit and miss attempts at finding gold and other mineral and natural resources, they stumbled upon plantation agriculture, as had been practiced in Europe for centuries. One crop in particular, tobacco, was found to be the great prize because it was indigenous to the New World. When Europeans tasted or smoked it, they were hooked, and a major, world-changing industry was born in the islands of the Caribbean. Demand soared, and supply could barely keep up. Arable land and a favorable climate were needed, as well as a labor force that could handle the work and the unhealthy conditions.

The whites learned early on that indigenous peoples in the Americas, for a variety of reasons—not the least of which was their lack of immunity to European diseases—did not make a good labor force. The Spaniards so abused and decimated the natives of the Caribbean, in fact, that Christian missionaries begged the government of Spain to find a new source of labor. Consequently, Spanish colonists soon turned to Africans. Equatorial and tropical Africans fit the bill perfectly for their needs. Coming from hot, humid, largely agricultural regions and having greater immunity to European diseases and (seemingly) to malaria, they appeared uniquely suited by nature for this specific task at this particular hour in history. By 1540, some 10,000 Africans per year were being shipped into the Caribbean colonies. Within another century, the Europeans had discovered that they could transplant sugar cane to the Americas, and a whole new cash crop industry was born, which increased the demand for African slave labor all the more.

A strange twist in this tale is that, immediately after Columbus's 1492 voyage of discovery, the Roman Catholic Church, which controlled both Spain and Portugal, prohibited Spain from engaging in the African slave trade that Portuguese entrepreneurs had pioneered. Therefore, to supply the labor needs of Spanish colonies, Spain had to rely on traders from other nations to bring them slaves. The consequence of this fact was that England and Holland were encouraged to enter the Atlantic slave trade. Following the pattern set by Portugal, these nations in the late 1500s and early 1600s competed for the Spanish *asiento* (the right to trade in slaves); in 1713, Great Britain obtained it exclusively once and for all.

By the turn of the seventeenth century, two notable developments had occurred. First, racism had been fermenting for more than 100 years already and was soon to displace all other factors as the primary reason for whites to single out Africans for slave labor. Second, England was ready to begin colonizing North America. That convergence of racist ideology and historical circumstance became the major development that would shape the next 230 years of American history and set up the conditions whereby a common practice of the Old World evolved into the "peculiar institution" of the mid-1800s in the southern United States.

Slavery and Abolition in the English Colonies of North America

The English established their first permanent colony in North America in 1607. They called it Jamestown in honor of King James I, who had recently taken the throne, and it was part of the larger Virginia territory as claimed by Sir Walter Raleigh for England some years before. When the colonists first arrived, they were mistakenly under the impression that they would be able to make money for themselves and their sponsor, the London Company, with a minimum amount of physical work. Five years and a dose of harsh reality later, they began experimenting with growing tobacco as a cash crop, and the age of hard physical work in the American South was thus begun. Tobacco, being a very labor-intensive crop, required more and more workers every year. The natural choice for a labor force initially was poor whites who voluntarily entered indentured servant contracts. So bleak were the economic prospects of many poor English families in the homeland that there was a constant supply of indentures to fill the labor needs of Virginia in those early years. Yet these white workers did not make an efficient labor force for the long-term needs of the colony, for a variety of reasons, including the fact that they often were intractable and had a high propensity for walking off the job and disappearing into the wilderness before their contracts expired.

In 1619, a Dutch ship brought the first Africans to Jamestown, where English colonists bought them. These Africans, and the next few boat loads of human cargo, were given indentured servant contracts just the same as whites. They were not singled out at first as something different despite their complexions. They became merely part of the multicultural milieu that was the American colonies. Within one generation, however, that had begun to change. It simply proved more convenient to stop giving contracts to Africans—a group of people who looked different and thus could not easily escape; were not Christians, could speak very little English, and thus could be disciplined harshly with a lash rather than corrected with mere words; and as a result, seemed much more pliable as a whole than the intractable whites. In 1661, therefore, Virginia established the status of African slaves as permanent by law. A year later, the colonial government added that the status of children born to slave mothers, regardless of who the father was, would be that of permanent slaves.

In 1672, another major development occurred when the Royal African Company was chartered in England. Its sole purpose was to make money off the Atlantic slave trade. By that time, there were several more English colonies in mainland North America that served as markets for slaves. Maryland, just across the Chesapeake Bay from Virginia, had the same basic economic conditions and thus the same labor needs. It legally recognized permanent African slavery a year after Virginia.

Farther south, the new Carolina colony became the first to be established with a legal recognition of African chattel slavery from its inception. Four of the original eight proprietors of Carolina were stockholders in the Royal African Company who stood to gain personally from promoting slavery. As a proprietary colony, Carolina's main purpose for existence was to make money for the proprietors, and any legal means of doing it was considered acceptable. The Carolina government actually encouraged settlers to bring slaves into the colony by offering free land on generous terms for each head brought in. Because these settlers generally intended to engage in plantation agriculture, they had every reason to take the offer.

Over time, Carolina split in two, with the southern half (with its favorable coastline and clear, fertile low country) continuing the original pattern of plantation slavery and the northern half (with its dangerous coastline and different, difficult topography) becoming largely an afterthought for all but the poorest settlers. The North Carolina colony never fostered the extreme caste system of its southern counterpart, although it, too, allowed slavery all along.

The last of the original 13 English colonies that eventually coalesced into the United States was also the one located the farthest south. It was Georgia, founded in 1732. Despite the original prohibition against slavery in the Georgia colony, all of the topographical and economic conditions that made South Carolina such a slave-holding center also prevailed on the south side of the Savannah River. By 1750, Georgia had become a virtual copy of South Carolina, having rescinded its prohibition against slavery.

Meanwhile, at mid-century in the 1700s, north of Maryland, slavery could be found in proportion to the economic conditions and labor needs of each individual colony. Not surprisingly, the smallest number of slaves (about 500) was counted in New Hampshire, the northernmost of the 13 colonies. Every other colony had at least 1,000 slaves. New York, with its burgeoning metropolis of Manhattan, boasted more than 11,000, which amounted to one slave for every six whites. Massachusetts had 4,000, which worked out to about one slave for every 44 whites. South of Maryland, every colony far exceeded those ratios. Virginia counted the largest number of slaves at just over 100,000, but South Carolina had by far the largest percentage—the slave population stood at more than sixty percent of the total and outnumbered the white population nearly two to one!

From the moment the first colony began to single out Africans for permanent slavery, there was something peculiar about the form that the institution took in America. Never before in human history had a group been singled out specifically because of race or color alone for slavery. To make that change, there had to be an assumption on the part of whites that blacks were naturally inferior beings. Scarcely can modern minds imagine any other rationale that could have brought about this important transformation. Although in retrospect the change appears dramatic, to those living at that time, it did not appear so. Indeed, the change was both subtle and gradual. Nor was it uniformly applied from colony to colony, much less slave holder to slave holder. Considering that white indentured servitude continued for many decades after the introduction of Africans into the colonies and realizing that both white and black slaves could still be seen laboring side by side well into the 1700s, it should not be surprising that the change did not come with a trumpet blast heralding its arrival. Only in time, over a matter of years, did the change really become noticeable on a large scale.

South Carolina was the first place where it became starkly manifest. As early as 1686 (just 20 years after the founding of the colony), South Carolina passed its first Slave Code for limiting the amount and type of freedom slaves could enjoy within the confines of their condition of servitude. Later, in the colony's upgraded 1712 Slave Code, the government gave a rationale for its limitations, saying that Africans were by nature savages that were completely wild and barbaric and thus unfit to be governed by laws and customs intended for whites. The theory of racial distinctions suddenly had taken a sharp turn for the worse.

At the same time, little antislavery sentiment was expressed anywhere, but that which existed was extremely important. In 1688, in a German community of the Philadelphia, Pennsylvania, area, a group of Friends (Quakers) led by Francis D. Pastorius issued the Germantown Protest, which became the first antislavery manifesto in American history. These men of Moravian descent, who came out of the Anabaptist-Mennonite branch of the Protestant Reformation, seemed to be alone in having prescient knowledge about the evil that was inherent and ever-growing in African slavery. Perhaps their own religious group's experience as victims of persecution made them more sensitive to the plight of the slaves because no other group of Protestants—Lutherans, Calvinists, or Anglicans—took a stand against slavery. Even so, the English Quaker majority in Philadelphia rejected the views expressed in the "Germantown Protest," so there certainly was no widely held antislavery sentiment in the denomination as a whole.

Although many Quakers continued to own and trade in slaves throughout the Colonial Era and into the Early Republic Era, more and more of them turned against slavery with each passing year. In 1693, a Quaker named George Keith furthered the abolitionist cause by publishing *An Exhortation and Caution to Friends Concerning the Buying and Keeping of Negroes*. Quakers were not the only ones who voiced opposition to slavery. Samuel Sewall, a Massachusetts magistrate who had previously become infamous for his role in the 1692 Salem Witch Trials, published an antislavery essay in 1700 called *The Selling of Joseph*, which argued against the notion that was already becoming prevalent in the late 1600s of blacks being naturally inferior and thus suited to slavery. Sewall contended that the fact that Africans longed and ached for freedom like white Englishmen proved they were just as human and just as much in need of liberty and justice as those who claimed superiority over them.

In 1711, the Pennsylvania legislature actually outlawed slavery, which seemed to be validated as a wise decision when in the following year the Africans in the colony just to the north, New York, staged the first slave revolt in American history (which itself validated what Sewall claimed). Yet, the colonial government of Pennsylvania was overruled by the imperial government of Great Britain, which gained the *asiento* in 1713 and thus stood to make fortune upon fortune from the slave trade. The British South Sea Company became the main purveyor of the slave trade under this new arrangement—it transported the bulk of the 6 million Africans who were shipped to the New World in the eighteenth century.

The effect of such heavy-handed governing from across the ocean served to agitate the antislavery Quakers. (Likewise, this and similar actions would ultimately lead Thomas Jefferson to blame the pernicious presence of slavery in America on the British government in the Declaration of Independence in 1776, although the final draft omitted it.) In 1729, a Philadelphia Quaker named Ralph Sandiford published an antislavery document called *A Brief Examination of the Practice of the Times* through none other than young Benjamin

Franklin's press. (The antislavery ideology would grow on Franklin over time until, by the 1770s when he became one of the Founding Fathers, he had developed into a full-fledged abolitionist.) In 1732, an English Quaker named Benjamin Lay moved to America after spending a couple of enlightening years in the extremely brutal plantation society of Barbados. Emerging a decided abolitionist, he published *All Slave-Keepers that Keep the Innocent in Bondage* in 1737 and spoke out against slavery at the Quakers' annual convocations in Philadelphia.

Another Englishman who moved to America in 1732 was the founder of the Methodist Church, John Wesley. In what came to be known as the Great Awakening, he and other revivalists—most notably George Whitefield—traversed the colonies converting non-Christians and lukewarm Christians to enthusiasts of the faith. Strongly opposed to slavery, Wesley made his imprint in the southern colonies, but it was not nearly great enough to offset the proslavery tradition there. Whitefield's greatest impact came in the northern colonies. In Philadelphia, for example, he made a true believer out of the somewhat skeptical or half-hearted Christian Benjamin Franklin.

While antislavery sentiment grew steadily in Pennsylvania, the number of slaves grew even greater in South Carolina, and the institution became even more entrenched there. Despite the colony's Slave Codes, the slaves as a whole actually had a generous amount of freedom to move about and to enjoy leisure time in the early 1700s, when measured against the harshness of slavery in later decades. This comparative leniency in enforcing compliance with the Slave Codes contributed to the outbreak of the second great slave revolt of the Colonial Era—the Stono Rebellion of 1739. It started on a Sunday morning after a night of drinking and discussing the possibility of a revolt. What began as a small group of slaves intent upon marching from the Charleston area to the Spanish territory of St. Augustine, Florida, morphed into a roving band of at least 60 men. Not a secret rebellion (like those that would occur in the 1800s), this group marched with fife and drum, announcing their intentions all along the way. Local whites formed a militia to put a stop to the march. In the end, 21 whites and about 100 blacks lay dead, and South Carolina passed another, stricter Slave Code in 1741 as a result. In that same year, slaves conspired in New York to burn down the town on lower Manhattan island. The important point to note about these revolts—and, in fact, all slave revolts in American history—is that they showed slaves themselves to be among the first abolitionists, as Samuel Sewall had claimed, rather than willing victims of bondage as proslavery ideologues charged.

Meanwhile, the Quakers in and around Philadelphia kept up their vocal opposition to slavery. Following on the heels of Benjamin Lay came John Woolman. He was an itinerant Quaker preacher from New Jersey who, in 1753, published the first widely distributed antislavery tract in American history, *Some Considerations on the Keeping of Negroes*. He followed that with a second volume in 1762, which was published by Benjamin Franklin. He kept a journal documenting his day-to-day activities on the mission trail, which was published posthumously in 1776. In 1754, he teamed up with Anthony Benezet to write *An Epistle of Caution and Advice*. Benezet was a Philadelphia Quaker schoolmaster who taught blacks in his home until he could erect a school building for them. He taught famous black leaders James Forten, Richard Allen, and Absalom Jones while becoming the standard bearer for antislavery sentiment in Pennsylvania in the generation of the Founding Fathers.

Largely as a result of the efforts of Lay, Woolman, and Benezet, in 1758, the Pennsylvania Society of Friends took an official stance against slavery for the first time. Not satisfied with this victory, they campaigned to outlaw slavery throughout the colonies and the British Empire. Benezet published *Observations on the Inslaving, Importing and Purchasing of Negroes* in 1759 and *A Caution and Warning to Great Britain and Her Colonies on the Calamitous State of the Enslaved Negroes* in 1766. His student William Dillwyn followed in his footsteps, publishing *Brief Considerations on Slavery* in 1773, before moving across the Atlantic to live in England.

For most of the Colonial Era, there was little distinction between America, England, or any other part of the British Empire with regard to slavery. In 1772, however, there being no compelling reason for continuation of the institution in a land full of poor whites with little plantation agriculture, slavery was effectively abolished in the British Isles under English Common Law by the case of *Knowles v. Somersett* (although it would not be abolished throughout the empire officially until 1833). There was a great paradox in the fact that the government which became the greatest purveyor of evil by maintaining the foreign slave trade should also be the first to abolish the institution within its local domain, leaving slavery as an orphaned legacy to the future United States.

Slavery in the United States: A Pernicious Problem for the Early Republic

In the early 1770s, colonial America's collective attention began to be focused more and more on the problems that would ultimately lead to 13 colonies declaring independence—imperial taxation without parliamentary representation; the nuisance of British soldiers, tax collectors, naval patrols, and other agents of the crown in America; and growing resentment manifest through revolutionaries calling themselves the Sons of Liberty. Although slavery seems in retrospect to have been virtually a non-issue amid this backdrop of history, it was certainly *the* issue to the slaves themselves. At the outbreak of the Revolutionary War in 1775, there were approximately 600,000 slaves spread over the 13 colonies. About 25,000 of them fought in the war—some 10,000 on the American side and 15,000 on the British side. Another 55,000 took advantage of the chaos and simply ran away during the war.

Throughout this time of turmoil, some white Americans found ways and means to continue their abolitionist activities. The legislature of Pennsylvania, for example, discussed ways to limit slavery, such as by doubling the tariff on imported slaves, which had the support of influential non-Quakers Ben Franklin, Benjamin Rush, and Thomas Paine, all of whom were about to distinguish themselves as Founding Fathers of the United States. Anthony Benezet and Paine, meanwhile, founded the Pennsylvania Society for the Relief of Free Negroes Unlawfully Held in Bondage in 1775, which was reorganized in 1784 as the Pennsylvania Society for Promoting the Abolition of Slavery but that was often called simply the Abolition Society.

Paine, perhaps the most truly democratic and egalitarian thinker alive at the time, published an article in the *Pennsylvania Journal* in 1775 called "African Slavery in America," which he followed with a pamphlet called *A Serious Thought*, in which he called the slave trade the worst kind of "traffic" conceivable to the mind of man. As the ink was still drying on that document, he was busy penning his monumental *Common Sense*, which was more responsible than any other single factor in convincing the 13 colonial governments to declare independence. Nor did his attention wane from the slavery issue even during the Revolutionary War that raged in North America until 1783. In the midst of it, Paine authored the preamble to the Pennsylvania Act for the Gradual Abolition of Slavery, which took effect in 1780 and made Pennsylvania the first American state to put an end to the institution.

Abolitionist activity also existed elsewhere besides Pennsylvania at this time. In 1776, a Congregationalist minister from New England named Samuel Hopkins published *A Dialogue Concerning the Slavery of the Africans*. He would go on in 1784 to lead Rhode Island to pass a gradual emancipation law and in 1789 to found the Rhode Island Society for Promoting the Abolition of Slavery. Massachusetts effectively, if not technically, ended slavery in 1783. Connecticut passed a gradual emancipation law in 1784. New Hampshire, New Jersey, and New York came on board within the next few years. In 1785, Alexander Hamilton and Aaron Burr, who later would be forever bound together in history by their infamous duel in 1804, led in creating an abolition society in New York. Vermont, which became the fourteenth state in the United States, was the first to adopt a constitution that expressly prohibited slavery from the start. It set the few slaves still living there free immediately. By the turn of the nineteenth century, there was essentially an uninterrupted land of liberty stretching from the Mason-Dixon Line (the border between Pennsylvania and Maryland) to Canada. When these seven American state governments passed laws officially abolishing slavery, they were the first in world history to do so.

Abolition in Massachusetts is particularly interesting because it resulted mainly from a series of court cases popularly known as the "Quock Walker" cases. Walker had been a slave in the Bay State who had been promised freedom by his owner. That owner died, however, before he could manumit Walker. The new owner then refused to honor the promise, so Walker ran away. He was captured and then beaten for having fled. He responded by suing the owner for assault. The Massachusetts Supreme Court found in his favor.

The ruling became a bell weather showing that public opinion was changing in the state. It showed that the judicial system there was (and probably would be from then on) sympathetic to slaves, not to owners, in interpreting the Massachusetts constitution.

As the tide was turning toward abolition in the Northeast, the main concern of the young United States as a whole in the 1780s was ensuring that this new nation that had been conceived in the Revolutionary War would be able to survive the peace that ensued thereafter. The nation's first government had taken the form of a "Continental Congress," which in turn had adopted a constitution called the Articles of Confederation and Perpetual Union. This constitution concentrated most of the actual governing power in the states rather than in the Continental Congress. This allowed each state to make its own laws about slavery, the result of which was, as previously noted, that all the northeastern states voluntarily began abolishing it. Yet no southern states followed their lead. The most notable piece of national legislation that came out of Continental Congress was the Northwest Ordinance, which stipulated that no future state created out of the Northwest Territory (north of the Ohio River and east of the Mississippi River) would be allowed to have slavery. This prevented Ohio, Indiana, Michigan, Illinois, and Wisconsin from ever becoming burdened by the cancer of slavery in the first place. Modern observers can only wonder how differently American history would have turned out had Congress been able to pass a complementary "Southwest Ordinance" to keep slavery out of Alabama, Mississippi, Tennessee, and so on. But it was not to be.

In 1787, a revolt of rural farmers against the high taxes levied on them by the state of Massachusetts—Shays' Rebellion—rocked the foundation of the United States. It precipitated the calling of a Constitutional Convention in Philadelphia to discuss ways to improve the Articles of Confederation so it could render the national government more effective at dealing with crises like this. In the midst of the convention, a majority of the delegates decided that rather than revising the current constitution, it would be preferable to write a completely new Constitution and create a "federal" government to replace the "Confederation." The resulting debates and final product became the stuff of legend.

James Madison, who emerged as the "Father of the Constitution," was a Virginia slave holder. Like his mentor, Thomas Jefferson (who did not attend the Constitutional Convention), he was an intellectual, an Enlightenment rationalist, and a deeply religious man. He was consequently apologetic about owning slaves, having inherited them. Yet also having become accustomed to owning them all his life, he never manumitted his slaves, not even in his will. He was somewhat conflicted over slavery, therefore, and he did not focus much on the issue during the debate, being overwhelmed with the bigger task of assembling the whole new U.S. Constitution (and soon the Bill of Rights). Even so, unavoidably, slavery briefly arose as a topic of discussion. In the end, Madison was careful never to use the word "slave" or any of its derivatives in the Constitution, partly out of shame and partly out of prudence. He hoped to avoid drawing attention to the metaphorical "elephant in the room."

The most contentious aspect of the discussion of slavery at the convention was determining how to count the slaves for purposes of congressional apportionment. Northern delegates generally opposed counting southern slaves altogether, saying that because slaves were not citizens of the states in which they lived but were instead deemed "property," southern states should not be allowed to benefit in the number of congressional representatives from their head count. Southern delegates vehemently disagreed, of course. Madison proposed that a bicameral Congress be created in which one house would represent free people only and the other represent the combined free and slave population. Although this proposal did not pass, it led to the "3/5ths Compromise," which has been one of the most misunderstood things in all of American history. Contrary to popular misconception, it did not calculate the value of the life of a slave at just over half of the value of a white person's life. Instead, it simply allowed southern states to count 60 percent of their slave populations toward congressional representation. It actually limited the damage caused by the pernicious problem to the new nation, but unfortunately, in hindsight, not nearly enough.

The 3/5ths Compromise was not the only way the new Constitution dealt with slavery. Another compromise placed a limit on the amount of time that slave traders legally had remaining to import slaves from Africa and other foreign sources, capping it at

20 years. By January 1, 1808, said the compromise, it would from thenceforth be illegal to import slaves. The purposes were to notify slave traders well in advance and allow them to wind down their businesses, discourage others from going into that line of work, and send a message (if only a vague and subtle one) that the gradual abolition of slavery was underway in the United States. Clearly the Southern apologists envisioned the scaling back of the institution over the rest of their generation and hoped for its ultimate abolition within another generation. Madison, Jefferson, and several others would live long enough to discover that they were mistaken. A third stipulation pertaining to slavery in the Constitution concerned fugitive slaves. It sought to deal with a specific problem that was looming at that moment and would undoubtedly continue to be a problem for years to come. Under the Articles of Confederation, with each state having sovereignty and relying on comity for the enforcement of its laws in interstate disputes, there was already a disagreement between Virginia and Pennsylvania over blacks in the strip of land around Wheeling (today in West Virginia). When Pennsylvania abolitionists rescued a black man claimed by a Virginia slave holder, it set off an ugly conflict between the two states that dragged on until after the Constitution was ratified. Then the first attorney general, Edmund Randolph (a Virginian), in the cabinet of the first president, George Washington (another Virginian), got stuck with the issue. After studying the problem, the Washington administration recommended legislation to Congress to deal with such cases. The result was the Fugitive Slave Act of 1793, which made it easy for slave holders to reclaim runaways. They merely had to make their claim in the local court having jurisdiction and offer a minimal proof of ownership. Slaves, not being citizens, did not get the benefit of a trial by a jury of their peers but were solely at the mercy of the presiding judge. They had no option of appeal. The law also set a fine of $500 for those convicted of harboring fugitive slaves.

Clearly, it was important to the first leaders of the federal government to protect the rights of slave holders, not the rights of slaves. Thus, it was left up to the northern states, inasmuch as they had power, to look out for the welfare of blacks. Hence, one by one after 1793, they passed "Personal Liberty Laws" designed to limit the effectiveness of the Fugitive Slave Act. The result was an ongoing competition between certain state governments, which used a states' rights interpretation of the U.S. Constitution, and the U.S. government, which used a national sovereignty interpretation. This seems ironic in hindsight because the South is commonly regarded as the section of the country that believed in states' rights. In addition to official state actions, however, some individual abolitionists and antislavery groups took it upon themselves to help fugitives regardless of the law. Isaac Hopper, a Philadelphia Quaker, was among the first to make it his life's mission to help slaves escape. He began operating what might be called the forerunner to, or an early version of, the "Underground Railroad." This issue of fugitive slaves and the Underground Railroad would simmer on the backburner until it would finally boil over in 1842 in the case of *Prigg v. Pennsylvania.*

In the meantime, foreign affairs grabbed attention away from slavery and other domestic issues when the French Revolution erupted in 1789. Dragging on for the next decade, it would usher in sweeping changes in the world that would have dramatic effect on the young United States: France and Great Britain would go to war, the United States and France would engage in a "quasi war," Napoleon Bonaparte would step onto the pages of history, the United States would wage the War of 1812 against Great Britain, and not until 1815 would the Western world see peace again. In the midst of all this tumult, the slaves of France's largest colony in the Caribbean waged a successful revolt in 1791, leading to the creation of the independent nation of Haiti and to France's abolishing slavery throughout its empire in 1794. Had this revolt not occurred amid all the other foreign affairs distractions, it likely would have caused the American government to pause, reflect on its own slave situation, and possibly change courses. It was not to be, and on the last days of the century in December 1799, free blacks in Philadelphia could be seen petitioning the U.S. government unsuccessfully to put a stop to the foreign slave trade eight years early.

Although foreign affairs stole most of the attention in the 1790s, events were transpiring in the American South with little notice that would have monumentally important and horrific consequences and cause the pernicious problem to evolve into the peculiar institution. In 1792, Eli Whitney, a man from Connecticut who was hired as a tutor on a plantation in the Georgia low country near Savannah, applied Yankee ingenuity to the problem of separating the seed from the lint in cotton and thus invented the cotton engine, better known as the "cotton gin." A simple contraption in hindsight, it revolutionized agriculture in the South, making cotton a far more lucrative crop than it had ever been before. It led to a demand for more slave labor to cultivate cotton in the Deep South. To fill the demand, foreign slave-trading firms, which would otherwise be out of business after 1808 by constitutional mandate, evolved into domestic slave-breeding companies, and a whole new, highly profitable industry was born.

To make a proverbial perfect storm for increasing the need for slave labor, two other things were happening at the same time. One, the Mississippi Territory was being opened to settlement, and its Natchez District offered some of the best land in the world for growing cotton, which led to a wave of agribusinessmen starting plantations and becoming millionaires using slave labor. Consequently, these rich cotton planters would be among the first great defenders of the institution of slavery rather than apologists for it. The lifestyle they created would become dubiously synonymous with the antebellum South in popular perception.

Two, the Industrial Revolution, which had begun in England in the mid-1700s, had hit the northeastern United States by the turn of the century. Steam-powered textile factories employing thousands of poor immigrants sprang up in Boston, New York City, Philadelphia, and surrounding areas. Northern industrialists (Lords of the Loom, as they were called) thus made their millions proportionate to the southern planters (Lords of the Lash), while northern financiers and shippers profited handsomely from the overseas cotton trade and while the poor white northern working class became dependent on an even poorer black Southern labor force for their own livelihoods. This was a marriage made in hell as far as the institution of slavery is concerned. These northerners who profited indirectly from slavery, although generally keeping a low profile on the issue, nevertheless became tacit defenders of slavery just as the planters became its outspoken defenders.

Around the turn of the nineteenth century, little discussion of abolishing slavery could be found in the United States, but what there was could be seen most vividly in the new Western states in

Appalachia. In the mountains of Kentucky and Tennessee, a burgeoning abolition sect sprang up, owing largely to the outbreak of the Second Great Awakening there. The Reverend David Rice tried to convince the delegates at Kentucky's constitutional convention to weave a prohibition against slavery into that state's very fabric, but to no avail. His speech, "Slavery Inconsistent with Justice and Good Policy," became such a powerful abolitionist statement, however, that others would publish and reprint it for mass consumption throughout the country. In 1808, Reverend David Barrow created the Kentucky Abolition Society and soon after began petitioning the U.S. government and influential Americans such as Thomas Jefferson on the issue. However, Rice and Barrow were in the minority in Kentucky, and both were ousted from the Methodist church. By 1815, the majority opinion in Kentucky could be seen in the state legislature's appeal to neighboring northern states, Indiana and Ohio, for their help in catching and returning runaway slaves.

Meanwhile, in the heavily proslavery tidewater region of Virginia, a slave rebellion led by Gabriel Prosser broke out, and in the New Orleans area, another one called the German Coast Rebellion occurred. Rather than convincing slave holders or their state governments to abolish slavery, these rebellions merely caused the South to become more strict and harsh in controlling their black populations. This increase in oppression coincided with the new business of slave breeding to make American slavery more degrading to the black race than it had ever been before. It became, in fact, dehumanizing. It was at this point, in the early 1800s, that the transformation of slavery from a common practice to the South's "peculiar institution" really began to manifest. Subtle and gradual, the change had begun. Few had noticed, and even fewer, it seems, had cared. The devolution was far from complete, however. In the coming decades of the 1810s to 1820s, slavery's Southern apologists would wane and die out, and a whole new generation of ardent defenders would arise to replace them. This devolution would in turn cause a backlash, creating more and stronger abolitionists. A geographical and ideological polarization of America would then ensue that ultimately would not be stopped by anything short of a tragic civil war.

TWO

The Emergence of a National Movement: 1816 to 1840

Antecedents: Gradual Emancipation, Manumission, and the American Colonization Society

The end of the War of 1812 and the Napoleonic Wars in 1815 ushered in a new era of both world and American peace. For the first time in its existence, the young United States could turn its attention to pressing domestic issues without being overly distracted by foreign affairs. Quakers, such as Isaac Hopper, Roberts Vaux, and Benjamin Lundy, continued their religious group's tradition of pressing for legal abolition nationwide using the strategy of moral suasion. By working on the consciences of the nation's lawmakers, attempting to shame southern slave holders into manumitting their slaves, and convincing more of the northern people that abolition was the will of God for America, they hoped to get gradual emancipation laws passed in the South like northern states had already adopted. The idea behind this gradualist approach, which was taken for granted in those days as the only orthodox view, was that evolutionary change was preferable to revolutionary change to prevent an overwhelming disruption to society and dislocation to individuals and families—white and black, free and slave alike. In addition, so the thinking went, slaves should be educated in preparation for freedom before being emancipated.

The question was how gradualism could be accomplished. One option was that states could pass laws to be put into effect at a later date—much like the foreign slave trade clause in the U.S. Constitution—thereby allowing slave holders adequate time to make arrangements for living their lives without unpaid labor and for helping set up their former workers in self-sustaining livelihoods. This plan, which would work like an indentured servant contract, managed to gain a great deal of traction among abolitionists in Great Britain over time, but it never caught on in the United States. A second option was to pass laws freeing all children born to slave mothers after a certain date, which would do nothing about liberating current slaves but would guarantee that the next generation of white children and black children would grow up together without the problem of slavery. One downside to this option would be the awkward familial and societal relationships produced by a whole generation of free black children growing up in slave environments and dwellings. Clearly, gradualism posed complex questions.

Gradualism actually could have been accomplished if some plan had been devised that a majority of Americans embraced for compensating slave holders for their financial loss. Compensated emancipation generally involved some type of government intervention in which tax money would be redistributed. Because the American people as a whole were constitutionally conservative and the United States' capitalist economic system fostered rugged individualism, such redistributive schemes were a hard sell. That did not prevent some political leaders from offering them, though. Various possibilities for compensated emancipation had been thrown around in discussion for decades. Levi Hart of Connecticut put forth the first one for his home state in 1775, but it was not adopted. In 1790, Elbridge Gerry of Massachusetts proposed a national plan to be paid for with revenue generated from the sale of public lands, which was likewise unsuccessful. In 1819, former President James Madison unsuccessfully reiterated the same basic plan. In the 1850s, a National Compensation Society was even formed to coordinate some such plan. The idea continued to be discussed well into the 1860s, right up to the middle of the Civil War. In 1862, Congress actually passed a $300 per slave compensation bill for the District of Columbia, but President Lincoln issued the Emancipation Proclamation and rendered a national compensation law unnecessary. Because compensation schemes were so difficult to achieve, abolitionists relied on the willingness of apologetic slave-holding individuals to work with them to find practical ways to achieve gradual emancipation. For slave holders who were compliant, there were several options: (1) they could allow their slaves to work for wages on the side, keep a portion of the money, save up the funds, and buy their own freedom after a matter of years; (2) they could allow some concerned third party, such as a wealthy philanthropist, an abolition society, or a church group, to purchase their slaves' freedom; (3) they could set their slaves free after they reached a certain age; and (4) they could liberate their slaves in their wills.

Each of these options was taken by individuals from time to time throughout the history of American slavery, but complicating factors surfaced in the early to mid 1800s that made such cases increasingly rare. For one, free blacks posed a unique problem for state governments, even in the northern states. Just because a state believed that slavery was bad did not mean the citizens believed racial equality was good. In fact, the opposite was generally true, such that there was really no place for free blacks in a white society; they would automatically be deemed inferior to whites and thus treated with disrespect by a majority of whites. As a result, Black Laws, which created social, political, and economic segregation, sprang up in the North as the counterpart to Slave Codes in the South. To the true egalitarian minority—most of whom were Quakers at the time—getting the slaves freed was thus merely a first step; the burden of changing hearts and minds to live up to the creed stated in the Declaration of Independence that "all men are created equal" still lay before them.

A second complicating factor was that most northern states required that former slave holders pay for the upkeep of their freed slaves to ensure that they did not become mendicants or otherwise burden the communities in which they resided. Southern states generally required manumitted slaves to leave the state within a matter of months. Where they were supposed to go was not specified, and that left them to fend for themselves in a hard world that offered them no welcome.

Considering this myriad of vexing problems associated with manumission and gradual emancipation, it is not surprising that foreign colonization of the black population ultimately became the most fashionable potential solution. No sooner had the War of 1812 ended and freedom of the seas been restored than a free black Quaker shipbuilder from Massachusetts named Paul Cuffe (or "Cuffee") started transporting fellow free blacks to Africa. Within two years, a group of white political and religious leaders that included President James Monroe, former President James Madison, Speaker of the House Henry Clay, and Chief Justice John Marshall, among many other famous southerners, formed the American Colonization Society (ACS) in Washington, D.C. Elected the first president of the ACS was George Washington's nephew, Bushrod Washington, who was a justice of the U.S. Supreme Court and, like most of the other ACS members, a slave holder.

Collaborating with the U.S. government, the British government, and African tribal chieftains, the ACS established the nation of Liberia on the west coast of Africa to be the designated place for colonizing free blacks from the United States. In 1820, it settled its first group of colonists there. By 1830, it had settled more than 1400, and within another two years, some 32 American states had endorsed the ACS and its Liberia mission. From the beginning, however, the ACS was plagued by problems. First, it relied on white slave holders to manumit their slaves voluntarily, which would prove a difficult proposition throughout the organization's history. Few took the ACS up on its offer. This should not be surprising considering that some ACS leaders did not lead by example in this regard. Bushrod Washington, for instance, who had inherited George Washington's substantial Mt. Vernon estate, kept his slaves until his death in 1829, never freeing them, not even in his will.

A second, related problem was that the ACS mainly relied on philanthropy rather than tax money to accomplish its mission, and there was never enough money to fill the need. A third problem was that most slaves, although certainly wanting their freedom, did not want to be shipped across the globe to the land of their ancestors—a place they had never been, knew little about, and that held more fear than charm for them. A fourth, related problem was that some free black spokesmen were suspicious of this predominantly southern white organization's motives, believing the real intention was not to look after the best interest of blacks but simply to rid the United States of them. In this camp were James Forten and Richard Allen of Philadelphia, later to be joined by Samuel Cornish, Henry Bibb, and many others. Although it took a few years for most white antislavery advocates to come around to that way of thinking about colonization, many eventually did.

Just as the ACS experiment was getting off the ground, the nation's first crisis involving slavery as a political issue struck. It was the Missouri Controversy of 1819–1820, and it was destined to have far-reaching ramifications for American history. Indeed, it would be, as Thomas Jefferson described it at the time, "a fire-bell in the night" to awaken the nation about the perilous issue of slavery. It began in 1819, when the Missouri Territory applied for admission as a slave state in the Union. The application was pregnant with geographic, political, and ideological tensions. Accepting Missouri's application would put it in league with the South despite Missouri's being farther north than most other slave states. It would temporarily upset the balance of power in the U.S. Senate between free and slave states. It would also make Missouri the first state admitted to the Union completely west of the Mississippi River, potentially paving the way for the rest of the old Louisiana Purchase Territories to become slave states in the future.

Two congressmen from New York, James Tallmadge, Jr., and John W. Taylor, led the opposition. Tallmadge came up with some sound political reasons to block Missouri's application, including the notion that the ill feelings produced by the bad relations between many masters and slaves could be used by foreign foes to weaken American defenses. Because the United States was barely five years removed from the War of 1812, this argument carried a great deal of weight, yet it did not carry the day for long. The Speaker of the House, Henry Clay of Kentucky, a slave holder and leader of the ACS, responded with the theory of "diffusion." He believed that allowing slavery to spread westward would diffuse the institution throughout more of the country, thus diluting its strength in the South and making the possibility of gradual emancipation more likely. Taylor disagreed, saying it would essentially double the demand for slaves, and it would dissuade white immigrants from moving west.

Interestingly, Taylor was elected Speaker of the House in 1821 and presided over the final debate on the bill. After the idyllic parliamentary standard of the Speaker's not playing an active role in the debate but merely presiding dispassionately instead, Taylor watched the bill pass via the Missouri Compromise: Missouri was admitted as a slave state, no other slave states would be admitted that far north in the Louisiana Territory, and Maine would be sliced off of Massachusetts and admitted as a free state to balance out the Senate. Although the crisis was averted for the time being, the alarm had been sounded, and the United States would never again have the luxury of falling back into its golden slumber. Slavery as a geopolitical issue was here to stay.

The Movement Is Born: Immediatism, Christianity, Women, and the American Anti-Slavery Society

The Missouri Controversy, along with the Denmark Vesey slave revolt plot of 1822 in Virginia, temporarily increased the ACS's prospects for success because more Americans than ever began to see the urgency of solving the slavery problem. Despite all of the problems the ACS faced, many people clung to the hope that some type of colonization scheme could be devised and phased in slowly over time that would extirpate the land of slavery while causing a minimum amount of disruption to both the individuals involved and to society as a whole. But events out of any white American's control conspired against it. For one, a growing abolition movement in Great Britain was making its way to the United States, mostly in the form of literature and newspaper articles and curiously at the hands of women rather than men. Most important in this category was Elizabeth Heyrick's *Immediate, Not Gradual Emancipation*, which was published serially in Benjamin Lundy's *Genius of Universal Emancipation* in 1825. It served to open the eyes of many American antislavery advocates and convert them to immediate abolitionism with no concern for whatever disruption may occur to society or individual lives.

The timing of Heyrick's writing was unusually propitious because it coincided with and helped nullify the effect of *A Plan for the Gradual Abolition of Slavery in the United States Without Danger of Loss to the Citizens of the South* (1825) by Frances "Fanny" Wright. A Scottish visitor to the United States, Wright had published *Views of Society and Manners in America* in 1821. In so doing, she became the first in a series of foreign visitors who enjoyed fame for writing observational documentaries about life in the United States over the next few years, including Alex de Tocqueville, August Beaumont, and Harriet Martineau—each of whom wrote scathing critiques of the peculiar institution in the 1830s. In 1826, Wright tried to implement her plan by founding an experimental Utopian community for free blacks near Memphis, Tennessee, called Nashoba. Its quick failure, as well as the fact that Wright became notorious as a "free love" advocate in the United States, ensured that her plan would not be taken seriously by mainstream Americans.

The 1820s also saw the rise of American women to positions of leadership as social reformers for the first time. Not surprisingly, Quakers in Philadelphia charted the course for others to follow. Lucretia Coffin Mott had been ordained as a Society of Friends minister in 1821, had joined the radical Hicksite sect of Quakers in 1827, and then helped start what came to be known as the Free Produce Movement in 1829. Her husband, James Mott, a wealthy cotton trader, boycotted southern cotton, which was grown with slave labor, and began trading in wool instead. Other conscientious northerners joined suit, which helped some, such as silk importers Arthur and Lewis Tappan of New York, to become fabulously wealthy by providing alternatives to cotton. At the same time, Benjamin Lundy began including a "Ladies Repository" section written by Margaret Elizabeth Chandler in his paper the *Genius of Universal Emancipation*. This practice would soon be copied by other abolitionist publishers, opening a whole new venue for female participation in the movement that was about to break forth in the land.

Of more urgent importance than any of the aforementioned factors in putting abolitionism front and center in the American public eye was the publication of David Walker's *Appeal to the Colored Citizens of the World*, which appeared in 1829. A free black from Boston, Walker encouraged slaves to rise up in violence and throw off their chains of oppression. Coming just a few months after the inauguration of Democrat President Andrew Jackson of Tennessee and Vice President John C. Calhoun of South Carolina— the first truly unapologetic slave-holding administration in American history—Walker's *Appeal* hit the nation with the impact of an ideological nuclear bomb. As copies of his book began to circulate in the South, southern state officials put a bounty on his head. Georgia, for example, offered $1,000 for him dead and $10,000 for him alive. Urged by friends to flee to Canada, he refused. Within the year, he was dead. His official cause of death was listed as consumption (tuberculosis), but conspiracy theories of his assassination have nonetheless circulated ever since. In seeking to unravel the mystery of Walker's death, the most likely scenario is that he knew his health was rapidly deteriorating and his death was imminent, and he wanted to speak his mind before he left this world. Because his days were numbered anyway, he had little to fear.

At the same time, a young white Boston-based Baptist named William Lloyd Garrison was busy trying to make a name for himself as an antislavery reformer. Following his mentor Benjamin Lundy, editor of the *Genius of Universal Emancipation* and founder of the *National Anti-Slavery Tract Society*, Garrison got his start in the business by writing for and editing small newspapers before striking out on his own in 1831 with his weekly newspaper printed in Boston called the *Liberator*. Having evolved from a gradualist and colonizationist to an immediatist by that time, Garrison determined to become the loudest and most incessant voice abolitionism had ever seen. He would ultimately achieve that objective but with many trials and tribulations in the process.

Because Lundy was focusing his efforts largely on converting southerners in and around Maryland and on federal lawmakers in Washington, D.C., Garrison decided to carve out his own niche by making it his personal mission to convert the people of New England to abolitionism. As he noted in the inaugural edition of the *Liberator*, he observed more opposition and contempt, as well as more racial prejudice and apathy, about slavery in the North than in the South. At first glance, that notion seems to smack of hyperbole, especially considering that Garrison had recently served a jail sentence in Baltimore for his abolitionist writings. Time would prove the veracity of Garrison's words, however, because he would personally endure a nearly successful attempt on his life in Boston and because several other abolitionists would suffer abuses ranging from being pelted with eggs to being murdered in cold blood in the North.

In the summer of 1831, while the nation was still abuzz from Walker's *Appeal* and had barely been introduced to Garrison's *Liberator*, the largest and most dramatic slave revolt in American history occurred in Virginia. It was led by a religious mystic slave named Nat Turner, who believed he was a modern-day Moses— God's chosen instrument for bringing about the liberation of his people. Instead, his actions resulted in the deaths of 200 people, including himself. His rebellion also caused the rift between the North and South, and the abolitionists and the proslavery people, to widen. Moreover, his rebellion quickly resulted in all southern states cracking down more stringently than ever before with Slave Codes designed to make a formerly oppressive institution even more diabolically harsh.

In the immediate aftermath of the Nat Turner rebellion, the political leaders of Virginia held a public debate among themselves about how to prevent such calamities in the future. Governor John Floyd favored passing a gradual emancipation law similar to Pennsylvania's. Notably, Thomas Jefferson's grandson, T. J. Randolph, supported the plan. They anticipated that most slave holders in the Old Dominion could be convinced to sell their slaves to ready buyers in the Deep South cotton kingdom. It would not solve the nation's slavery problem, but it would solve Virginia's, and that was their main concern. Virginians were largely divided over the issue by social class and geography, with the wealthy planter elite of the Tidewater opposing emancipation and their poorer counterparts in the Piedmont and Appalachians favoring it. The planter elite carried the day; there would be no end to slavery in Virginia. Instead, the state's slave holders would begin to tread the path already being beaten by Vice President Calhoun and others—they would stop apologizing for slavery, hunker down, and prepare to defend their peculiar institution at all costs, calling it a "positive good" for the South and indeed the nation. Thomas R. Dew's *Review of the Debate in the Virginia Legislature of 1831–1832* (1832) documented this episode and showed the direction the proslavery argument would take.

As these developments were occurring in Virginia, a series of events were happening elsewhere independently of one another yet all complementing one another. For one, the British abolition movement was achieving its zenith, as Parliament was debating, and about to pass, the Abolition of Slavery Act, which had a tremendous ripple effect across the ocean, encouraging American abolitionists to amp up their own efforts. William Lloyd Garrison answered the call, making a full frontal assault on slavery by forming the New England Anti-Slavery Society, publishing the *Liberator* as well as his anti-ACS manifesto *Thoughts on Colonization*, and lecturing on immediatism throughout the North. Another who answered the call was Elizur

Wright, Jr., a professor at the Western Reserve College in Cleveland, Ohio. He published a book in 1833 whose title came to epitomize what the abolition movement would stand for from then on: *The Sin of Slavery*. It announced a change that was already well underway by the early 1830s but that had not been in sharp focus— the abolition movement was essentially a Christian religious crusade.

Indeed, by the early 1830s, various Protestant denominations, independent churches, and ministers—Congregationalists, Presbyterians, Methodists, Baptists, and Unitarians, among others—were now ready to join forces in large numbers and share the burden of leadership with the Quakers to make abolitionism the social reform issue of their generation. Because the purpose of the crusade was to stamp out a grave sin, there could be no delay. Gradual emancipation could not possibly suffice. Immediatism was the only way to go, for surely it must be God's way. Unavoidably, abolitionism would thus become the domain of religious radicals and zealots. At least that is what they would appear to be to the majority of Americans in both the North and South. In their own minds, they considered themselves merely people who took the Christian Golden Rule literally and seriously: those who would not choose to be slaves themselves should not make slaves of others.

Among the true believers in the gospel of immediatism were the wealthy Calvinist businessmen from New York City, Arthur and Lewis Tappan, who began organizing the New York Anti-Slavery Society in 1833. Garrison and the Tappan brothers, who had first met in 1829 when the latter bailed the former out of jail in Baltimore, wasted no time in joining forces with each other and then reaching out to the more established Quaker antislavery societies in Pennsylvania to create the American Anti-Slavery Society (AASS) in December 1833. Its constitution stated its *raison d'etre* succinctly: "The object of this Society is the entire abolition of Slavery in the United States." Its Declaration of Sentiments laid out a laundry list of supporting reasons for the necessity of its creation that stemmed mainly from the Bible and the U.S. Declaration of Independence.

The establishment of the AASS was one of the high-water marks in the history of the abolition movement—this organization would play a central role in the fight to destroy slavery from then on. Nearly every person who would leave his or her mark on the movement for the next three decades, with a few notable exceptions, would be a member of it at one time or another. Indeed, its roster reads like a who's who of American abolitionists. Of its 60 charter members, 57 were white, and three were black. All were men; women were initially allowed only to observe, not participate. The role of women in the AASS would be a topic of debate from the beginning but would emerge as one of the two major bones of contention leading to the organization's rupture by the end of the decade (the other would be whether abolitionists should launch their own political party).

Garrison and the Tappan brothers' purpose in creating the AASS was simple: they wanted to bring together all abolitionists and all antislavery societies in the United States, allowing them to pool their resources in terms of money and talent and thus facilitate their collective ability to speak out against slavery with a unified voice. Although its mission, methods, and membership would evolve over time and eventually cause it to splinter, it was amazingly effective for a few years at achieving its original objective. By 1838, it boasted more than 1,300 state and local chapters that together claimed a membership of about 250,000. The organizational structure was weak, however, because each unit was semi-autonomous, regionally focused, and thus only marginally concerned with national directives.

One of the ironies of abolitionism is that, by the time the all-male AASS was created in 1833, the movement had already begun to spread like wildfire at the grass roots level through the establishment of "female" antislavery societies, such as the one founded by Lucretia Mott and Mary Ann McClintock in Philadelphia. Within five years, nearly every city and town of any size in New England had one, and there were no fewer than 40 in Massachusetts alone. The role of women in the movement cannot be overstated. Nor can the effect that participating in such a public, grass roots social reform campaign had on fostering what would ultimately become the women's rights movement. The abolition movement and women's rights movements were in fact destined to be intertwined inextricably for the next three decades.

The year 1833 also hosted some important antislavery publications by writers who would play leading roles in the movement thereafter.

The Quaker poet John Greenleaf Whittier burst forth as a national figure with *Justice and Expediency*, as did the husband and wife team of David Lee and Lydia Maria Child with *The Despotism of Freedom* and *An Appeal in Favor of That Class of Americans Called Africans*, respectively. Whittier also helped Garrison write the Declaration of Sentiments for the AASS. Whittier would go on to achieve greater fame as the author of two books of abolitionist and egalitarian poetry, *Poems* (1838) and *Voices of Freedom* (1846). David Lee Child did not greatly distinguish himself in the movement after 1833, although not for lack of effort. He supported the Free Produce Movement by attempting unsuccessfully to start a northern free labor sugar beet industry to replace slave-grown cane sugar. His wife "Maria" Child did distinguish herself, however, as one of the most prolific of all abolitionist authors. In 1835 and 1836, she published *Authentic Anecdotes of American Slavery*, *The Anti-Slavery Catechism*, and *Evils of Slavery and the Cure of Slavery*. The husband and wife team of the Childs also served as editors of the *National Anti-Slavery Standard* in the 1840s.

While all this activity was taking place in New England and the Middle Atlantic states in the early 1830s, there was a burgeoning abolition movement taking shape out on the western frontier. In 1834, Lane Theological Seminary in Cincinnati, Ohio, which had only been in business for about five years, became ground zero for arguing over the direction of the abolition movement when it hosted a series of public debates on slavery and abolition. Most of the students, who were followers of the revivalist Charles G. Finney theologically and of William Lloyd Garrison and the AASS philosophically, seemed more radical in their abolitionist views than the administration of the school. Lyman Beecher, who had come from Boston to serve as the seminary's president, although very much an antislavery advocate, had to try to balance out the conflicting views of his students and his board. He did not approve of the radical abolitionist agenda. After a falling out, a group of students, led by Theodore Dwight Weld, left the seminary and headed to northern Ohio to enroll in Oberlin College, a new school that had the financial backing of the Tappan brothers of New York, among other philanthropists.

Oberlin, which hired Finney as its professor of theology in 1836 and as its president in 1851, would prove fertile ground for radical abolitionism for the first three decades of its existence. It would also become the first coeducational college in the United States, which would make it equally fertile ground for the concomitant women's rights movement. Many of its "Lane Rebels," as they were called, were employed as "agents" of the AASS to take the gospel of abolitionism throughout the Midwestern frontier of Ohio, Indiana, Michigan, and beyond. Lane itself would continue to prosper under Beecher's conservative regime. In an ironic twist of fate, Beecher would see two of his children, Henry Ward and Harriet, go on to eclipse him in fame, both becoming radical abolitionists who would play central roles in the movement in the 1850s.

Although the question of the role of women had been present during the first two years of the AASS, it was not until 1836 that it began to be a major, divisive issue. That is when an enthusiastic young lady named Angelina Grimke wrote a letter to Garrison expressing her hatred for slavery. Not only was it an articulate, impassioned, and reasoned statement, but it came from the daughter of a South Carolina slave holder who had first-hand knowledge of the peculiar institution! Angelina, along with her older sister, Sarah, had converted to the Quaker faith and moved to the North and joined the Philadelphia Female Anti-Slavery Society. Garrison was so taken by her letter that he published it in the *Liberator*. Thus, the first female star, so to speak, of the abolition movement was born. The Grimke sisters penned three impressive abolition pamphlets over the next two years and progressed from lecturing before exclusively female audiences to speaking to mixed audiences of men and women.

Some of the more sexually conservative members of the AASS, such as the Tappan brothers, did not approve of this intermingling of the women's rights issue with the abolition issue, but they did not immediately take a strong stand against it. Garrison, Elizur Wright, Theodore Weld, and Henry Stanton, however, were among the leaders of the AASS who not only accepted women as equals but encouraged them to play a greater role in both the abolition movement and in protesting for women's rights. Weld did not merely support Angelina; he even married her, which eventually led to her, ironically, stepping back from taking a leadership role in the movement to be a wife and mother. The Weld–Grimke alliance produced one of the greatest publications of the whole abolition movement, *American Slavery As It Is* (1839), which represented the most scathing indictment of the peculiar institution yet written. It showed from actual southern newspaper reports the cruelty and inhumane nature of slavery as it existed in the 1830s, which helped convert thousands of northerners to the cause.

After the Grimke sisters set the pattern for women lecturers, other women soon followed their lead. In 1838, Abby Kelley of Massachusetts, speaking before the Anti-Slavery Convention of American Women, so impressed Weld that he invited her to become a national lecturer, which she did in 1839. For the next 15 years, she would go on to exceed Angelina as an orator and star. She, rather than the Grimke sisters, would ultimately be the one to cause the great schism in the AASS in 1840.

The Backlash to the Abolition Movement in Society and National Politics

A major development in the history of abolitionism was the backlash of violent retribution it produced in American society and the legislative retribution it produced in American politics. To begin, most white northerners in the 1830s were not abolitionists. Indeed, the majority considered abolitionists a group of fanatics whose religious beliefs had twisted their racial views. They thus saw it as their duty, in some cases, to protect their communities from infiltration by abolitionists and in other cases to keep the abolitionist activism tamped down to an innocuous minimum.

One of the first cases of violence aimed at an abolitionist that made its way into the history books was the Prudence Crandall affair in Connecticut. Crandall was a Quaker who founded the Canterbury Female Boarding School. She advertised in the *Liberator* her intention to enroll black students in April 1833. Some townspeople reacted negatively to this news. The state government even passed a law to prevent her from legally carrying out her plan. She was arrested, tried, and convicted of violating the law. She continued trying to teach, however, until an angry mob descended upon the school, broke the windows, and hurt some of the students. She then closed the school and left the state, never to return and never to play a leading role in the movement thereafter. Although she had been more of an educational egalitarian than an abolitionist per se, her strongest support came from radical abolitionists, and her opponents did not make such distinctions between these two complementary varieties of fanaticism (as they deemed it) anyway.

The year 1834 saw the vandalism of Lewis Tappan's Brooklyn, New York, home by a mob protesting his abolitionist activities but was otherwise a mostly quiet year. 1835, however, witnessed a spate of anti-abolition riots and mob attacks. The most notable case was a riot that erupted in Boston where an English abolitionist named George Thompson was scheduled to speak to the Massachusetts Female Anti-Slavery Society. Seeing a rowdy mob gathering outside the hall, Thompson wisely chose to keep his distance. William Lloyd Garrison was not so fortunate, however, and he became the scapegoat. The mob caught him, tied a noose around his neck, and seemed intent upon lynching him until he managed to escape.

At about the same time, a mob surrounded the home of Paulina and Francis Wright in Utica, New York, determined to burn it down. The Wrights were targeted for organizing an antislavery conference. The only thing that saved them and their home was that they and a few other women knelt and began praying loudly and fervently, which shamed the mob into inaction. They subsequently moved their conference to the home of Gerrit Smith, a man destined to play a large role in the movement in coming years. Meanwhile, in an unrelated incident down in Nashville, Tennessee—the hometown of President Andrew Jackson—Amos Dresser was tried, sentenced, and publicly scourged for merely possessing abolitionist literature.

The violence continued into 1836, when a mob attacked the New Haven, Connecticut, home of Simeon Smith Jocelyn. A founding member of the New England Anti-Slavery Society, he had also founded the local New Haven Anti-Slavery Society in 1833 and had supported Prudence Crandall. Around the same time in Montpelier, Vermont, Samuel May was assaulted by a mob. A Unitarian minister who earned his theology degree at Harvard, he, too, was a founding member of the New England Anti-Slavery Society and a strong supporter of Crandall. He also served as an agent and secretary of the Massachusetts Anti-Slavery Society. Likewise, Jonathan Blanchard, one of the so-called "70 agents" of the AASS, was scorned and assailed by more than one mob for lecturing and distributing abolition literature in western Pennsylvania from 1836 to 1837. Henry Stanton claimed to have been targeted on at least 70 occasions in the Ohio–western New York corridor. Such atrocities were only the beginning of sorrows.

In 1837, the most infamous case of violence against an abolitionist in the history of the movement occurred in Alton, Illinois, when Elijah P. Lovejoy was murdered by a mob. Lovejoy had moved to St. Louis at the time of the Missouri Controversy to work against Missouri's admission to the Union as a slave state. Failing, he moved back east, attended Princeton Theological Seminary in New Jersey, and was ordained by the Presbyterian Church. In the early 1830s, he returned to St. Louis and began publishing a newspaper that aroused the ire of the proslavery locals. Thinking it safer to move across the Mississippi River into the free state of Illinois, he soon discovered that not to be the case. When his press was destroyed by vandals on more than one occasion, the Ohio Anti-Slavery Society helped him replace it each time. Again thinking there would be safety in numbers, he marshaled some of his 2,000 subscribers and formed a new antislavery society in the area. Barely two weeks later, however, he found himself and a small group of supporters fighting off another mob determined to destroy his press. In the ensuing gunfight, he was killed.

The murder of Lovejoy ushered in a new phase of the abolition movement. Thousands of Americans who had previously not been much concerned with the slavery issue were awakened to the seriousness and urgency of the problem. These new converts included some who would become indispensable to the movement over the coming years, such as Wendell Phillips of Boston and Gerrit Smith of upstate New York. It was a mixed blessing for abolitionism. On the one hand, it helped swell the ranks of the AASS and its affiliates by provoking sympathy, but on the other hand, it prompted proslavery advocates to accuse abolitionists of instigating mob violence through their radical activism. At the time, the latter was still more persuasive than the former. Likewise, at the time, the women's rights issue was still just as unnerving to the rank and file of the American people as the abolition issue. Not surprisingly, therefore, in 1838, at a women's meeting held to dedicate Pennsylvania Hall in Philadelphia, a mob descended upon the building and smashed its windows and the following day set it ablaze. Reminiscent of what happened five years earlier when Prudence Crandall continued teaching even as her school was pelted with rocks and other assorted missiles, Angelina Grimke kept her poise, continued talking, and finished her speech as scheduled.

Just as there was much anti-abolition sentiment in American society in the 1830s, there was much in the U.S. government as well. After the War of 1812, the United States had temporarily been more politically united than at any other time in history. The two-party system had collapsed, and one party calling itself the National Republicans had emerged. In the midst of this so-called Era of Good Feelings, some major political issues arose that were destined to destroy the delicate harmony. One was the aforementioned Missouri Controversy. Another was a reform issue called Universal White Male Suffrage, which swept across the land in the 1820s and gave poor white men the right to vote in most states for the first time. A third was the contentious presidential election of 1824, in which John Quincy Adams of Massachusetts and Henry Clay of Kentucky had joined forces to defeat Andrew Jackson of Tennessee. Jackson and his followers called the political deal that created the Adams–Clay alliance the "corrupt bargain," and they determined to ensure that President Adams and Secretary of State Clay got only one term in office.

For the Jacksonians to accomplish their plan of unseating Adams and Clay in the election of 1828, they created the Democrat Party in 1825 and courted the newly enfranchised poor white voters, who overwhelmingly flocked to the side of the great military hero of the War of 1812, Andrew Jackson. They won the election handily, and the Democrats then dominated the next three decades of American politics, making this the so-called Era of Jacksonian Democracy and the Age of the Common Man.

Although there were some antislavery people among the Democrats, such as the New Yorker and founding father of the party Martin Van Buren, the majority were either proslavery or apathetic about slavery. As a rule, the southern members of the party were, or soon became, vehement defenders of slavery, but the northern members had joined the party for political and economic reasons that had little to do with slavery one way or the other. These northern allies of the South and its peculiar institution would, in time, come to be known as "Doughfaces," and they would play a leading role in trying to stop the abolition movement.

The emergence and success of the Democrat Party and the strong-handed presidency of Andrew Jackson in the late 1820s led to the reactionary development of the Whig Party by 1832. Headed by Adams, Clay, and Daniel Webster of Massachusetts, they would be as close to an antislavery party as America would see in the 1830s, although they would be more divided over the issue than the Democrats were. By the 1840s, a faction calling itself the Conscience Whigs would emerge and become one stronghold of abolitionism. Abolitionists lacked any semblance of unity, however. Some, led by William Lloyd Garrison, did not favor political involvement at all because they considered the U.S. Constitution a proslavery (and hence a satanic) document, but others, led by the Tappan brothers, wanted to create a whole new political party devoted to no other issue but abolitionism. Considering this wide diversity of opinion, it is no wonder the movement struggled to gain political momentum for so long.

Amid this backdrop of history, in the mid and late 1830s, a torrent of events thrust abolitionism front and center into the spotlight of national politics. First, the AASS began its so-called Great Postal Campaign. Funded mostly by the wealthy Tappan brothers, it cost about $30,000 in postage—an enormous sum at the time—and involved more than one million pieces of mail. The idea was to get abolitionist newspapers, tracts, and periodicals into the hands of as many influential Americans as possible and to do it as quickly as possible. Lewis Tappan considered this distribution of literature to be an example of following the Biblical admonition to sow the good seed of the Christian faith. Publications such as the *Liberator*, the *Emancipator*, the *Antislavery Record*, *Human Rights*, and *The Slave's Friend* were mailed to northern pastors in an attempt to win them over through moral suasion. Judging from the increase in subscriptions thereafter, this northern recruitment aspect of the campaign bore impressive results.

There was also a southern strategy inherent in the Great Postal Campaign, although barely 20,000 of the one million parcels were mailed to southern addresses. Of them, almost all were addressed to ministers, political leaders, and editors. Most never made it to their destination. Southern postmasters, with the blessing of the Jackson administration, a host of congressmen, and state government officials and local citizens alike, took actions to prevent their delivery. In Charleston, South Carolina, a mob even burst into the post office, seized the stack of abolitionist mail, and burned it along with effigies of Garrison and the Tappan brothers. President Jackson thereafter recommended that Congress pass a law to prohibit the U.S. postal system from shipping what he called "incendiary" materials. The Democrat majority in Congress, which generally followed in lock step with the commander-in-chief, demurred on this recommendation, however, preferring to keep the mail a states' right issue.

At the same time, in 1835, the Texas Revolution erupted. Texas had been a province of Mexico, which itself had only won its independence from Spain in the early 1820s. Mexico did not permit slavery within its borders, but many Americans who had settled in Texas disregarded that prohibition and held slaves in open violation of the law, extending the Deep South cotton kingdom ever farther westward. This, along with several other issues, led to a rift between the Mexican government and the Texans, which devolved into an all-out war that lasted about one year and drew the attention of the people and government of the United States. Proslavery Americans favored aiding Texas and annexing it into the Union; antislavery Americans did not. Thus, a political fight was on that would end up lasting nine years.

President Jackson supported annexation but was in his last months on the job and had several other important issues that kept him preoccupied. Because he had wielded more executive power than any president before him and had almost always enjoyed the support of a majority in Congress and of the American people, it seems likely that he could have brought Texas into the Union as a slave state if he had only had more time. His successor, Martin Van Buren, opposed annexation, but mainly because he considered it politically inexpedient, not so much because he felt intense moral compunction about expanding slavery to the West. Although Van Buren was an able politician and party organizer, he lacked the popular support that the great war hero Jackson had enjoyed.

A national economic depression started by the Panic of 1837 plagued his one term in office. He and the Democrat majority in Congress tried but failed to fix the problem. Voters blamed him and his party and rebelled in the midterm election of 1838 and the presidential election of 1840, which brought the Whigs to power for the first time.

At the outset, the young and energetic American Antislavery Society took advantage of the Texas issue, petitioning Congress against annexation and encouraging local chapters and individual members to do the same (as many female antislavery societies had been doing for several years already). It also petitioned for slavery to be abolished in the nation's capital, the federal city of Washington, D.C. Within one year, the AASS had generated some 30,000 petitions, flooding the congressional mails and immediately becoming a nuisance to proslavery and apathetic representatives and senators. To deal with the problem, the Democrat majority in Congress, led by Henry L. Pinckney of South Carolina, passed a resolution in 1836, after several days of heated debate, that came to be known as the "Gag Rule," which prevented such petitions from being read in the House of Representatives. (The Senate did not adopt formal resolutions but accomplished the same type of gag by more subtle, although equally effective, means.)

The Pinckney resolution was intended only for one session of Congress, but it was renewable by a majority vote in each session thereafter. Rather than causing the AASS to give up the fight, however, it caused the abolitionists to intensify their efforts—they sent some 130,000 petitions to Capitol Hill from 1837 to 1838. The Gag Rule was thus passed again for the next two years. Going into 1839, the Democrats, led by New Hampshire Representative Charles G. Atherton, strengthened the restrictions in the rule, refusing to allow the House even to receive antislavery petitions, much less have them read aloud or debated.

Not surprisingly, the Gag Rule met with stiff opposition from a vocal minority that believed it to be an unconstitutional restriction on First Amendment rights. Leading the opposition was John Quincy Adams of Massachusetts, the only former U.S. president ever to go on to serve in the House of Representatives. Adams was very much a champion of individual freedom, but he did not consider himself an abolitionist. In fact, similar to a majority of his fellow northerners at the time, he disdained the AASS as a bunch of religious radicals who were unnecessarily stirring up controversy and causing discord in America. Even so, he could not brook the silencing of one group of his fellow Americans by another. Therefore, he openly defied the Gag Rule on one occasion by presenting 350 petitions against slavery.

All the heavy-handed parliamentary tactics designed to silence the abolitionists ultimately backfired because many American voters who did not care greatly about slavery one way or the other and did not agree with John Quincy Adams on most other issues, nonetheless considered the Gag Rule to be an unconstitutional limitation on freedom of speech. This contributed to the Whig party's gaining a majority in the House for the first time in the election of 1838, although the Whigs, who were more divided over slavery than the Democrats, would not succeed at overturning the new rules until 1844.

THREE

Growing Pains of the Abolition Movement: 1840 to 1848

The Great Schism: Women's Rights, Third-Party Politics, and Foreign Affairs

The 1830s had been the first decade in American history in which abolitionism became a real and major social movement. It had brought the emergence of William Lloyd Garrison as the most notable leader of the movement. He was nothing if not eccentric. He held strong, if sometimes evolving and vacillating, views on an odd assortment of reform issues of the day—pacifism, temperance, and Sabbath keeping, just to name a few. He favored women's rights, and he did not merely give lip service to making reform in that area. He actively recruited female speakers for the American Anti-Slavery Society (AASS) and writers for the *Liberator* and lobbied for women to have equal membership with men, including the right to vote and to hold office in the organization. If that were not enough to make him a radical among radicals, his views had grown more anti–U.S. government and anti–U.S. Constitution each year that went by. He believed the free states should have no union with slave states, and because they currently did, he refused to vote in federal elections.

Garrison had been the driving force behind the creation of the AASS in 1833, and he was destined to remain a *tour de force* of the movement from then on. Yet by the end of the decade, Garrison's radicalism had caused dissension in the ranks of the AASS, which jeopardized its ability to speak as the collective voice of the movement. Going into the 1840s, the Tappan brothers, who, more than anyone else, bankrolled the AASS, had different ideas about the direction of the organization. Because they largely controlled the purse strings, they naturally believed they had the right to set

the tone and chart the course for the movement. The direction they
chose was diametrically opposed to Garrison's vision of "no union
with slave holders." They wanted abolitionists not only to vote
and not have to choose between the Democrats and Whigs, but to
have their own political party devoted to the cause of freeing the
slaves—a "Liberty" party.

The first serious mention of forming a third party came at an AASS
meeting in 1839. Garrison and those who agreed with his radical
stance outvoted the Tappan brothers and their comparatively moderate supporters. The verdict, however, did not deter the faction that
favored political activism. Rather, it caused them to put their plan
into action apart from the AASS. The leaders of the faction included
Arthur Tappan, Myron Holley, William Jay, Geritt Smith, and Salmon
P. Chase. They called a meeting in Warsaw, New York, late in the
year and began forming the Liberty Party. For president, they
nominated a rare southern abolitionist named James G. Birney,
who was a lawyer, newspaper editor, excellent public speaker, and
ironically, a slave holder up to that year. They nominated Francis
Lemoyne of Pennsylvania for vice president. Not catching the vision
for the party just yet, each man declined his nomination.

Still the party organizers were not deterred. In April 1840, they
called a national convention in Albany, New York. They nominated
Birney again, and this time he accepted. They added Thomas Earle
of Ohio as the vice presidential nominee. Birney, who had agreed
to run more from politeness to his supporters than from conviction
that he could win, did not campaign. Instead, he spent most of the
year abroad, speaking at abolition conferences in Great Britain. Not
surprisingly, in the November election, Birney and the Liberty Party
received only about 7,000 votes nationwide.

Meanwhile, the decision to enter the national political arena
despite the Garrisonians' objections, along with Garrison's insist-
ence on promoting women in the society, naturally caused the growing friction in the AASS to come to a breaking point. In preparation
for the May 1840 national meeting, Garrison urged his faction
(mostly members from Massachusetts) to attend in order to outvote
the Tappan faction. The strategy worked. When the meeting began,
Garrison pushed for the election of Abby Kelley to a seat on the
executive committee. With a vote of 557 to 451, Kelley, and hence

Garrison himself, won. It was the final straw. The Tappan faction, which numbered 294 initially, walked away from the AASS and immediately formed the American and Foreign Anti-Slavery Society (AFASS). Arthur Tappan was elected president, Lewis Tappan was elected treasurer, and James G. Birney and Henry B. Stanton were elected secretaries. Joshua Leavitt became editor of its newspaper, the *Emancipator*, and Lydia Maria and David Child edited its other publication, the *National Anti-Slavery Standard*. The Liberty Party would be its official political arm for the coming decade.

Despite the addition of the word "Foreign" to the title, there was little about the new organization that focused on non-American slavery issues. What the title really indicated was that the new group would stay in line with the orthodoxy of English abolitionism, which did not favor women's rights, which had already proven successful at transforming a whole empire by political activism, and whose main organization had a similar name—the British and Foreign Anti-Slavery Society. There was also a nod to the black refugees and freedmen of Canada, the West Indies, Liberia, and Sierra Leone in the title. In 1846, the Tappans and their auxiliary, the "*Amistad* Committee," would create the American Missionary Association specifically to focus on helping those and similar, generally destitute, black groups. Arguably, the AMA would ultimately become the most productive reform organization in nineteenth-century America, surviving long beyond the abolition of slavery and reaching more people in a positive way than any other association of its kind.

Garrison and most of his faction did not miss those who departed the AASS in any way except in terms of finances. They were rather glad to have complete control of the direction of the organization. One notable exception was John Treadwell Norton, a wealthy Connecticut merchant who had just recently been elected vice president of the AASS before the rupture. He tried to heal the rift between the two sides, but it was no use. Neither Garrison nor the Tappans were interested in making up. They were destined to go their separate ways permanently, each wanting the same thing but going about it differently.

Garrison and the AASS wasted no time in implementing their joint agenda of abolition and women's rights. They chose delegates and immediately set sail for England, where the first World Anti-Slavery

Convention was being held in June 1840. Upon arrival, Abby Kelley and Lucretia Mott were rebuffed by their all-male British hosts. Incensed, they walked out. Male delegates stayed and represented the AASS, however, offering the convention an analysis of the current state of affairs in the United States called *Slavery and the Internal Slave Trade in the United States*. A second world convention would be held in London three years later, but to avoid the whole messy fracas over women delegates, the British did not send invitations to the AASS but rather to the AFASS. The British knew that, for all intents and purposes, the politically active and ambitious AFASS, not the apolitical AASS, would now be the real standard bearer of the abolition movement in and after 1840. Besides, they were already working closely with Lewis Tappan and his faction to deal with the *Amistad* slave revolt case at the time, and the two worked well together.

As all this discord and reorganization of the movement was going on, major developments were occurring on other fronts. Most notably, the *Amistad* affair was brewing and would soon become the great issue of abolitionists on both sides of the Atlantic in 1841. The *Amistad* affair began on June 28, 1839, when a Spanish ship left one port in Cuba headed for another loaded with 53 slaves from West Africa. In transit, a slave named Joseph Cinque led a mutiny that put the ship in the hands of untrained navigators who hoped to sail to Africa. Drifting far off course, the ship actually sailed close to the North American coast and was intercepted by agents of the U.S. government who guided it to harbor in Connecticut in late August. There the mutineers were charged and jailed in the town of Farmington while they awaited trial. The Van Buren administration, up to its neck in economic and political issues, did not want the distraction of a federal case involving the *Amistad*. Abolitionists in and around Connecticut were determined to make it one, however, and they succeeded.

The *Amistad* case was not the first or last case involving slaves and ships on the high seas that captured the nation's attention. It was, however, the one that became the most important in relation to the abolition movement. The *Antelope* case of the 1820s had brought to the surface some unusually complex international financial issues to the U.S. Supreme Court because a determination had to be made about who had the right of recovery of lost property if slaves were stolen by pirates. It began when an American pirate ship stole some 281 foreign slaves with the intent of selling them. Spanish and Portuguese claimants presented claims in the American courts for their return or recompense. Because there was no thriving national abolition movement at that time, however, almost no one suggested that the slaves had any right of recovering their freedom. Because their legal ownership could not easily be established, the U.S. Supreme Court decided the case with a convoluted set of awards that basically appeased every claimant but did so at the slaves' expense.

The *Amistad* case was similar, but the major difference was that, by the 1840s, the abolition movement was now big enough and influential enough to affect the outcome. Two preliminary courts ruled in favor of granting the Africans their freedom in 1840, but the case was appealed to the U.S. Supreme Court. Meanwhile, at about the same time that he was helping create the AFASS and the Liberty Party, Lewis Tappan founded and, along with John Treadwell Norton, bankrolled the *Amistad* Committee, which recruited the venerable elder statesman John Quincy Adams to lead the defense of the mutineers at the bar of the U.S. Supreme Court. In the argument culminating in February 1841, Adams performed masterfully and succeeded at getting the Africans their freedom and a return trip to their homeland. The 35 survivors went home in November, and the *Amistad* Committee saw to it that they were taken care of thereafter. This effort became the genesis of the aforementioned American Missionary Association.

Even as the *Amistad* case was being adjudicated, a similar slave ship issue arose in October 1840. An American ship called the *Hermosa*, en route from Virginia to New Orleans with 38 slaves, wrecked in the British Bahamas. Local authorities seized the slaves and emancipated them, per British law, setting off a heated exchange between the U.S. government, which prosecuted the claims of its slave-holding citizens, and Great Britain. Relations between the two nations would be made even more tense a year later. In November 1841, an American ship called the *Creole*, carrying 135 slaves, also en route from Virginia to New Orleans, experienced a mutiny in which the slaves guided the ship to the Bahamas, whereupon they were likewise set free by local authorities, again to the consternation of the U.S. government and its slave-holding claimants. Not until the mid-1850s would these and other similar cases finally be collectively resolved via an international commission.

These cases showed the growing disconnect between the United States and the most powerful nation on earth, Great Britain, and the rest of the industrialized world, in terms of how they perceived slavery. Trend-setting nations, such as Great Britain and France, as well as other countries such as Mexico, had already abolished slavery. The Americans clinging to it and defending it was, in their opinion, becoming increasingly anachronistic with each year that passed. It made diplomacy more complicated than it had to be, and it set up numerous international conflicts in the 1840s and 1850s.

It seems that these foreign affairs problems that arose as the unintended consequences of slavery should have bolstered the cause of abolitionism and undermined the cause of the "slavocracy" (as John Quincy Adams called the proslavery forces that controlled the South and the U.S. government). Yet the opposite was true. Ironically, the fact that the United States pressured Great Britain into compromising and paying a large portion of the claims actually stoked the fires of the slavocracy in the years leading up to the Civil War. It padded the southern ego, inspiring even more intransigence than was already present in the South at that time. In the meantime, it spurred more abolitionist activism. Joshua Giddings, an Ohio Whig who in 1838 became the first true abolitionist ever elected to Congress, drew up the "*Creole* Resolution" in 1842, which asserted the right of slaves to rebel at sea. The proslavery and Doughface majority in the House of Representatives retaliated by censuring him. He resigned his seat in protest, but the voters of his district immediately reelected him and sent him back to Washington.

On the national political front, the Liberty Party grew rapidly over the first four years of its brief existence until it received nearly 63,000 votes in the presidential election of 1844, again with Birney at the top of the ticket. Although this represented a ninefold increase over its 1840 count, which would have made for phenomenal success in other walks of life, it was not nearly enough in national politics at the time because the two major parties were polling 1.3 million apiece. Ironically, the party of abolitionism had done what third parties have always done in American history, which they never set out to do—garner just enough votes to throw the election from the proverbial lesser of two evils to the greater. Henry Clay, a Whig who opposed the annexation of Texas and the expansion of slavery to the West, had been the odds-on-favorite to win, but he lost to James K. Polk, a proslavery Democrat from Tennessee who strongly favored annexing Texas and extending the grip of slavery westward.

Despite this undesired outcome, the Liberty Party persisted into 1846, by which time Polk and the Democrats had provoked a war with Mexico over the Texas issue. The controversial war added yet more members to the party, making it large enough to become, if it so chose, a coalition party rather than a single-issue party. In effect, it could have potentially developed into the replacement of the Whig Party, which would have offered voters a more stark choice in future elections and possibly could have radically altered the course of American history, although that is only a speculation. Members who favored taking this coalition option formed the "Liberty League" to advocate a broad array of reforms, but members who believed it best to remain focused on one issue at a time withstood this change. Hence, an irreparable rift was in the making, which combined with events related to the Mexican War to kill the party and bring on its replacement, the Free Soil Party, by 1848.

The Fugitive Slave Issue: The Underground Railroad, the Rise of Black Abolitionists, and Last-Gasp Attempts to End Slavery through Law and Reason

The Underground Railroad was a secret network of abolitionists who aided slaves in escaping their captivity in the South and finding freedom in the North or, in some cases, Canada. Partly because of its secrecy and partly because it evolved over time, historians have sketchy records to work with for its early years. Not until 1850 did abolitionists begin documenting individual slaves who managed to escape and the accomplices who helped them. William Still, a black Philadelphian, was the pioneer of this documentation. What we know for certain is that, going back to the late 1700s, there had always been a few Quakers, mainly in Pennsylvania, New Jersey, and New York, such as Isaac Hopper, who invested a great deal of time, effort, and expense in hiding runaway slaves. Not until the 1840s, however, was the network large enough to cause serious alarm in the South and thus draw national attention. Only then was the term "Underground Railroad" coined, supposedly by Charles Turner Torrey, one of its operatives in Maryland, to describe the network (although some sources cite an escape in 1831 in Kentucky as the term's possible point of origin). The terminology was timely because the invention of steam-powered locomotives and the concomitant building of actual physical railroad tracks had only happened the late 1820s and early 1830s. It was also descriptive because both the actual railroads and the so-called Underground Railroad were well-organized transportation networks for moving people long distances in a short time as safely and conveniently as possible. Both had "conductors" (people who took great pains to help slaves escape) and "stations" (homes, businesses, and churches where fugitives were hidden).

By the time the term was coined, most of the runaways and fugitive-hiding activities occurred in the West with slaves from Kentucky and western Virginia escaping to Ohio, Indiana, Illinois, and western Pennsylvania. The self-described "president" of the Underground Railroad in the West was Levi Coffin, a North Carolina–born Quaker who moved to the frontier in 1824 and helped start the Indiana Anti-Slavery Society. He spent much of his career in Newport (today Fountain City), but he moved from the Hoosier state to Cincinnati, Ohio, in 1847. Altogether, it is believed that he helped some 3,000 slaves escape over the course of his lifetime. Calvin Fairbank, a Methodist minister from New York who had graduated from Oberlin College, was perhaps the second most important conductor in the West. He appears as a tragic figure in history because he spent a total of 17 years in prison in Kentucky for helping slaves escape. John Rankin of Ripley, Ohio, a Presbyterian minister who had founded the Ohio Anti-Slavery Society in 1834, was also among the most famous and important of the conductors in the West. His house on a hill overlooking the Ohio River was a frequent stop on the fugitives' northward journey. It was there that author Harriet Beecher Stowe would later find much of her inspiration for the saga she bequeathed to the ages in her 1852 novel *Uncle Tom's Cabin*.

Supported by western abolitionist writers, educators, and politicians, such as Cassius M. Clay, John G. Fee, Hiram Kellogg, Jonathan
Blanchard, Benjamin Smith Jones, Oliver Johnson, Sheldon Peck,
Salmon P. Chase, and many others, Underground Railroad conductors moved untold thousands across the Ohio River and into Canada
via Detroit and Buffalo. By 1848, Canada was home to more than
5,000 fugitive slaves, who were permanently free as long as they
stayed; Canada had no agreement with the United States about
extraditing them or allowing them to be reclaimed.

Plenty of conductors could be found in the East, as well. Charles
Turner Torrey, a Congregationalist minister from Massachusetts
who William Lloyd Garrison converted to abolitionism in the 1830s,
operated in the Baltimore–Wilmington–Philadelphia corridor. He
helped perhaps 400 slaves escape before being caught, tried,
convicted, and sentenced to a six-year prison term in Maryland in
1844, where he died while incarcerated. His funeral was held in
Boston, however, and became an abolitionist rally. Thomas Garrett,
a Quaker, was another important conductor in the Wilmington,
Delaware, area. He is believed to have helped some 2,700 slaves
escape. In 1848, he was convicted in Maryland of aiding a fugitive
slave family and given a $1,500 fine, which was an enormous sum
in those days. (The most notable of all conductors in the East,
Harriet Tubman of Maryland, did not emerge on the scene until the
1850s, and, although she helped a comparatively small number
escape, she did it in dramatic fashion amid the most dangerous and
treacherous conditions.)

Occasionally, slaves attempted their escape not overland but on
ships at sea. In 1848, Daniel Drayton and Edward Sayres were caught
trying to smuggle slaves out of Washington, D.C., by way of the
Chesapeake Bay. Despite having the able legal counsel of Horace
Mann, who took John Quincy Adams's seat in Congress upon his
death and went on to be one of the great educators in American
history, Drayton spent four years in federal prison before being
pardoned by President Millard Fillmore. In such cases, although
technically not an Underground Railroad activity per se, shipping
and smuggling nonetheless became part of the bigger fugitive slave
problem that plagued the nation in the 1840s. By 1850, it had become
so enervating to slave holders that the slavocracy demanded and got

new and stronger legislation to guarantee redention (the capture and return of runaways to their legal owners).

Clearly, whether there had been an Underground Railroad or not, some slaves would have tried to escape anyway. Regarding the slave rebellions, it is evident that American slaves, despite proslavery defenses to the contrary, wanted freedom. The fear of severe punishment, perhaps death, if caught in the act was the greatest inducement not to run away. That, plus lack of knowledge about things that free, literate people understood—mainly geography, politics, and culture outside the South—kept the vast majority of blacks in mental bondage, feeling hopeless and forlorn in their condition. Even so, a small fraction of brave souls risked their lives to attain that illusive freedom, and the Underground Railroad was their greatest ally.

Of all the runaway slaves in American history, none is more famous or important than Frederick Douglass. He was not the first to escape to freedom and make a name for himself, but he made a bigger impact than any other and left a larger imprint on the pages of history. Born of mixed-race parentage with the given name of Frederick Bailey, he grew up mostly in the Baltimore area. With little help from any Underground Railroad operatives, he fled north in 1838 at the 20 years of age. Making it to New York, he changed his name to Douglass and began making acquaintances with abolitionists. He soon met William Lloyd Garrison, who was immediately smitten by his charisma, his rhetorical ability, and his life story. Garrison, who had previously secured other blacks such as Samuel Ringgold Ward and Charles Lenox Remond as lecturers for the American and the Massachusetts Anti-Slavery Societies, respectively, hired Douglass as an agent for the Massachusetts Anti-Slavery Society. His effect on audiences was the same as it had been on Garrison, except many observers questioned the authenticity of his story, thinking an untutored former slave incapable of such eloquence.

Douglass's growing celebrity meant he was not safe from capture as a fugitive. Consequently, he did not stay in the United States but traveled abroad on a lecture tour of Great Britain. Making friends and raising money there, he was able to buy his freedom. In 1845, he attracted more attention than ever, both national and international, when, against the advice of both Garrison and his chief lieutenant Wendell Phillips, he published his autobiography. It became a worldwide sensation and commercial success, and it put him on the path to becoming a writer for the rest of his career, which displeased Garrison, who valued him as a public speaker. Douglass's determination to print his own newspaper, the *North Star*, and his support of the politicization of the abolition movement via the Liberty and Free Soil Parties broke his relationship with Garrison irreparably in the late 1840s.

Although Douglass's autobiography became the classic among all slave narratives, it was not the first of its kind. As early as the mid-1830s, fugitive slaves began publishing their stories. *A Narrative of the Adventures and Escape of Moses Roper, From American Slavery* (1836) seems to have been the first. Douglass's success, however, ushered in a wave of publications over the next few years. William Wells Brown, James W. C. Pennington, Moses Grandy, Henry Bibb, Josiah Henson, Henry Box Brown, and Sojourner Truth were just some of those who capitalized on the opportunity. It may be that the explosion of slave narratives in the 1840s and 1850s was a natural occurrence that would have happened under any circumstances. It may be, however, that the phenomenon was merely a reaction to all the attention being paid to runaways because of high profile cases that split public opinion in the nation over the enforcement of the Fugitive Slave Law.

One of these high profile cases, *Prigg v. Pennsylvania*, was heard and ruled upon by the U.S. Supreme Court in 1842. Similar to virtually all cases that make it to the highest court in the land, it presented a complex legal question: what latitude do states have in passing laws dealing with fugitive slaves, if any, in light of the federal Fugitive Slave Act of 1793? Taking a states' rights position on this issue, Pennsylvania had previously passed two laws designed to protect fugitives from being captured and returned to slavery. The state law and federal law clashed when, in 1837, Edward Prigg, a hired fugitive slave catcher from Maryland, entered Pennsylvania to capture a female slave named Margaret Morgan. Prigg and his accomplices were arrested, prosecuted, and convicted under state law, but they appealed the verdict. The U.S. Supreme Court, run by Chief Justice Roger B. Taney, a Jacksonian Democrat who was a Maryland slave holder, not surprisingly overturned the verdict.

It would not be the last time Taney got tangled up with slavery as a constitutional issue leading to a controversial national policy; he would also rule infamously in the Dred Scott case in 1857.

Meanwhile, the 1842 case of George Latimer, a Virginia slave who was given asylum in Massachusetts in violation of state law, was even more provocative and compelling than the Prigg case. Abolitionists including Henry Ingersoll Bowditch, William E. Channing, and Frederick Cabot formed a group called the Latimer Committee to try to keep the law from taking its course. When Latimer's legal owner came from Virginia to Boston to seize him, the committee gathered nearly 52,000 signatures and sent it to John Quincy Adams in Congress, hoping to get a change in the law or at least to show the cruelty of the existing law. Frustrated by all the negative attention, Latimer's owner sold him to the committee for $400. The success of the Latimer Committee offset the Prigg ruling and emboldened abolitionists to continue their efforts to thwart the Fugitive Slave Law. Not all slave holders were so easily appeased, however, and the abolitionists would lose more cases than they would win over the coming years.

The 1847 case *Jones v. Van Zandt* arising in Kentucky illustrates the point. John Van Zandt of Ohio carried a group of slaves from the Bluegrass State across the river to freedom. Slave catchers representing the owner Wharton Jones went into Ohio and apprehended them and then charged Van Zandt with aiding and abetting fugitives. Thus, a citizen of Ohio was convicted under Kentucky law, which brought to light one of the sticky issues of the whole federal Fugitive Slave Law: it created bad neighbors among border states. Before this time, Kentucky and Ohio had relied on comity regarding fugitive slaves, but such voluntary cooperation was always tenuous. Van Zandt's defense team, led by Salmon P. Chase of Ohio and William Seward of New York, who would go on famously to become cabinet members in the Lincoln administration a few years later, took the case to the U.S. Supreme Court. Again, Taney and his proslavery majority ruled against the abolitionists.

The Van Zandt case has historic importance in two ways. First, it became, in a sense, the final straw leading to the drafting of a new Fugitive Slave Act in 1850. It showed that relying on comity would be impractical going forward because it would likely lead to ever more cases appealed to the U.S. Supreme Court. Second, it brought Chase and Seward, who had previously not known each other, together for the first time. They would make a strong legal phalanx for the abolitionist cause in the coming decade and strengthen the foundation of the new Republican Party in the late 1850s. In the meantime, it helped bring Chase more recognition within the movement, such that he was chosen to draft the platform of the Free Soil Party in 1848.

Another front on which the abolition movement continued to be waged in the 1840s was that of intellectual literature, particularly books dealing with theology and religion. In 1840, two important books came out that shook the foundations of the church world. One was James G. Birney's *The American Churches: The Bulwarks of Slavery*, published first in England and soon after in the United States, which excoriated the southern clergy for their defense of slavery. The other was Cyrus P. Grosvenor's *Slavery v. the Bible: A Correspondence Between the General Conference of Maine, and the Presbytery of Tombecbee, Mississippi*. Grosvenor, an officer in the AASS who resided in Massachusetts, goaded his own Baptist denomination toward a schism by publishing his book that simply contained a series of letters in which abolitionist Baptist leaders and proslavery Baptist leaders debated the biblical merits and demerits of slavery. Not exactly compelling reading material for the general public, it, along with Birney's much more titillating *exposé*, showed that the North–South polarization, which would ultimately lead to the Civil War in the 1860s, was already well underway by the end of the 1830s.

Grosvenor's book was followed in 1843 by a more provocative read, Stephen S. Foster's best seller, *The Brotherhood of Thieves, or, a True Picture of the American Church and Clergy*. Foster, a graduate of Dartmouth College in New Hampshire, had become an abolitionist in the early 1830s and had grown increasingly radical over time. He made his reputation—and many enemies—by disrupting northern church services to speak out about slavery. Whereas Birney and Grosvenor had shown the defects of the southern churches, Foster went after his fellow northerners. He held the majority of them in contempt for their apathy and complacency about the issue that he believed demanded the most urgent attention of any in the world at the time. (He also married Abby Kelley, the great female lecturer of the AASS.)

Such books did not cause the splitting of the two largest Protestant denominations in America—Methodist and Baptist—but they certainly contributed to the schisms in each group. The Methodist Church ruptured in 1844 over southern bishops owning slaves, which went against the denomination's official code. The proslavery Baptists broke away and formed the Southern Baptist Convention in 1845, which was destined to become the largest Protestant group in the United States in time. Even then, the abolitionists continued making a relentless attack on what they viewed as the hypocrisy of many fellow Christians. For example, William Goodell published *Come-Outerism, the Duty of Secession from a Corrupt Church* in 1845, and Grosvenor followed his aforementioned book with a similar tome in 1847, *A Review of the "Correspondence" of Messrs. Fuller and Wayland on the Subject of American Slavery*, which documented a debate between a minister from South Carolina and his counterpart from Rhode Island. In the same year, Parker Pillsbury, a Congregationalist from New Hampshire who was expelled from his own denomination for his outspoken views on slavery, published *The Church As It Is; or The Forlorn Hope of Slavery*.

By the time these books appeared, there was little new that could be said on the subject, which may largely account for the decline in the number of similar publications in the decade leading up to the Civil War. For that matter, most of the intellectual, philosophical, and theological ground that could be trod in the debate over slavery had surfaced at some point in the 1830s and had been written down and published in the 1840s. Most of the publications of the 1850s, therefore, focused mainly on preaching to the choir, so to speak, rather than on trying to win converts. There remained one area to debate, however—the U.S. Constitution. At about the same time that William Lloyd Garrison and his followers were proclaiming that document a product of Satanic influence, a Massachusetts lawyer named Lysander Spooner was writing *The Unconstitutionality of Slavery* (1845), which introduced a twist to the standard abolitionist interpretation of the Constitution. Spooner argued that the Constitution, similar to the Declaration of Independence, was a product of natural law. The original intent of the document (if not of every individual framer), he believed, was antislavery, not proslavery. Thus, the common interpretation that upheld slavery represented a corruption of what the document was really all about.

Spooner's treatise was too scholarly to appeal to most common folks, and it scarcely changed any minds. He went on to write *A Defense of Fugitive Slaves* in 1850, in which he maintained that civil disobedience to the unjust laws of the land was acceptable—an opinion that many northerners who never read his book already shared, and that the Boston Transcendentalist writer Henry David Thoreau had first put forth in 1849. He practiced what he preached, supporting the man who would take the abolition movement and the nation by storm in the late 1850s with his militant plans, John Brown. He parted ways with a majority of abolitionists during the Civil War, however, when he argued that secession was a constitutional right of the states.

Spooner makes an interesting case study in the history of abolitionism's evolution. His focus shifted from finding one last way to make an intellectual case that slavery was bad and wrong in the 1840s to essentially admitting disgust and defeat on that front in the 1850s and saying all that remained was to take up arms against it. In that respect, he precipitated the majority view within the movement in the decade leading up to the Civil War.

Arguing Over Slavery: Intellectual and Religious Attacks on Slavery and Proslavery Apologetics

If it is true that by 1850 there was basically nothing left to be said—if there were virtually no arguments remaining that could change any minds, and if action alone would now suffice—the end of the 1840s makes a good place to stop our narrative and recap the abolitionists' case against slavery and the pro-slavery apologists' response to it. At the end of the 1840s, both sides dug their ideological trenches and hunkered down in them in the years leading up to the Civil War and emancipation.

The abolitionists' arguments fell into two broad categories: religion and rationalism. First, the religious arguments: simply put, abolitionists said the Christian Bible condemned slavery. In the Old Testament, the story of Moses and the Israelites in Egypt seems to make it clear that God does not condone slavery. In this Bible story, the Israelite slaves were the good guys, and the Egyptians who held them captive were the bad guys. God destroyed Egypt for not letting his people go free. Indeed, whether one believes the story in the Bible from the Judeo–Christian point of view or not, history proves that Egypt began its steady decline as a great world power immediately after Moses led the Israelite labor force out of the land of the pharaohs. Abolitionists believed that the same thing would happen to the United States if it, as a nation, did not repent of the sin of slave holding or of tacitly approving the institution of slavery by failing to speak out against it.

Continuing with this religious theme, in the New Testament, abolitionists pointed to scriptures such as the "Golden Rule," where Jesus said to "do unto others as you would have them do unto you," and to "love your neighbor as you love yourself." They noted that many southern slave holders claimed to be Christians and asked how they could justify holding someone in captivity and still call themselves followers of Christ. To obey these teachings of Jesus, said abolitionists, slave holders would have to repent and set their slaves free. If they did not, God would surely bring destruction upon them just as he brought destruction upon the Egyptians. This argument proved quite prophetic because the Civil War did bring destruction upon the section of the country that tried to justify slavery. This religious argument was simplistic, and it was designed to work upon the moral consciences of slave holders. By the 1840s, it had lost its power, and it rarely penetrated the southern mind, which rapidly built a defensive wall against moral suasion.

The second category of arguments rested upon rationalism, and it was designed to work upon the intellect of slave holders. Rationalism was a philosophical worldview that had become prevalent in Europe and America in the 1700s. Rationalism spawned the era of world history known as the Enlightenment, and the Founding Fathers and the nation they created were both products of it. Rationalists rejected belief systems and traditions of the past, which were often based on unfounded superstitions and myths, and they formed new beliefs and practices based on what made the most sense to them intellectually. This led most of them to reject institutions that were thousands of years old, such as the Roman Catholic Church, as irrational and unnecessary carry-overs from an earlier time. The continued practice of holding human beings in perpetual bondage in the mid-1800s was clearly another example of the same—an institution that had its origins in an earlier, unenlightened time, which, consequently, had not stood the test of time.

The abolitionists pointed out in their second argument that, once this nation had passed through the Enlightenment, it could not now cling to and defend the outdated institution of slavery. To do so would be to reject the progress that humankind had made in the past century. The United States was too educated, too knowledgeable, too enlightened to take such a step backward toward barbarism and savagery. This idea that American slavery was a throw-back to the past rather than the wave of the future was based on the fact that it was a direct descendent of and thus a continuation of the old European feudal system in which an aristocracy owned all of the land but a peasant class that had no rights worked the land. Those European peasants of the past, similar to American slaves of the 1800s, had no social mobility. They were born poor and they died poor, unless, those peasants immigrated to the United States—then they would ideally enjoy "life, liberty, and the pursuit of happiness." This country was founded on the hope of betterment for all people, said abolitionists, not the belief that one group should permanently rule another group.

A third argument of the abolitionists, which also sprang from this philosophy of rationalism, rested on a tangible, political basis: the Declaration of Independence, the document that created the nation, which says that "all men are created equal and endowed by their Creator with certain unalienable rights, which include the right to life, liberty, and the pursuit of happiness." Abolitionists asked how slave holders could justify slavery in light of this egalitarian ideal embodied in the Declaration; the Founding Fathers obviously envisioned a land of freedom for all people when they created the United States. Abolitionists believed that proponents of slavery were perverting the original intent of the Founding Fathers. Slavery, said abolitionists, was at its core un-American, and therefore it was wrong and needed to be abolished.

A fourth argument of the abolitionists, which also sprang from rationalism, rested on the ideal of humanitarianism. Slavery was cruel and inhumane by its very nature. Even slave holders who were kind to their slaves in terms of providing for their physical needs still abused them emotionally and psychologically by holding them captive and not allowing them to pursue happiness in their own way. Then, of course, many slave holders were not kind to their slaves. Some treated their slaves no better than livestock, as if they had no feelings at all. There were too many cases where slave holders beat, tortured, and killed their slaves. There were too many cases where slave holders raped slave girls. Such rapes created half-white babies who were still considered slaves because they were born to a slave mother. There were too many cases where slave holders broke up slave families by selling children away from their mothers. There were too many cases where slaves died trying to escape to freedom, most of the time because they were trying to get to the place where their loved ones had been sold. A system that would allow such abuses of helpless men, women, and children was most inhumane.

Many variations on these general themes were hashed out over the years. Abolitionists did language studies, for instance, that showed how most of the King James Bible's references to slavery should have been translated to mean indentured servitude—which was morally acceptable—but the current American form of slavery was more like what the Bible called "man stealing" (kidnapping) or oppression of the poor, which were unacceptable. Even so, precious few new points were added to the basics of the abolitionists' arguments in the 1850s or 1860s. Those few points are important, however.

The defenders and proponents of slavery responded to the charges that abolitionists levied against them. They had an answer for each abolitionist argument, and over time, they developed more and better ways to combat abolitionism than merely playing defense. The basics of their defensive arguments on religion and rationalism were fairly well laid out in the 1830s and 1840s, but they built a well-articulated offensive case in the 1850s based on changing socioeconomic conditions and new quasi-scientific racial theories. These offensive ideological weapons were not so much new, however, as merely used more effectively in the 1850s. All of these arguments can be found packaged in a giant compendium called *Cotton Is King, and Pro-Slavery Arguments* ... compiled by E. N. Elliott of Mississippi in 1860.

Meanwhile, their religious response was simple: in reading the Christian Bible, they considered several passages of scripture on the subject of slavery besides the ones that abolitionists were fond of quoting. There was, for example, the fact that some of the greatest men of God in the Old Testament were themselves slave owners. Abraham, the patriarch of the whole Judeo–Christian world, owned slaves. Others owned concubines (female sex slaves who were not equal to wives but who were held for the purpose of having sex and having babies). Moses, the very man whom God chose to lead his people out of bondage in Egypt, had a concubine, as did Abraham. Why was it all right, asked the apologists, for men of God in the Bible to own slaves and sexual concubines but men of God today could not?

Continuing with this religious theme, the apologists also pointed to the New Testament. They noted the little book of Philemon, which was a letter written by Paul the Apostle to a slave owner named Philemon, who Paul referred to as a brother in Christ. In this letter, Paul addressed the issue of slavery. He said that Philemon's servant, who was named Onesimus, had run away from his master and had arrived at the apostle's doorstep. Paul told Philemon that he had instructed Onesimus to return home, and then he instructed Philemon to forgive his servant and be kind to him. Paul then told Philemon that when Onesimus returned, he was not supposed to punish him for running away but rather receive him as a brother in Christ. If God opposed slavery, said the apologists, why would the Apostle Paul have not simply demanded that Philemon let his servant go free? Other New Testament scripture passages that seem to indicate that slavery was an accepted institution even within the early Christian church were also favorites, such as verses that say: "Are you bound? Seek not to be free . . . ," "Servants, obey your masters . . . ," and "Let every person be subject to the governing authorities, for there is no authority except from God. . . ."

Regarding the philosophy of rationalism and the Enlightenment, the apologists pointed out that the European feudal system had served as the vehicle by which the Anglo-Saxon people had been able to rise to democracy over a matter of centuries. It was a necessary evil, they said, because it had given plenty of time for the peasants of Europe to learn, grow, and finally become worthy of the high calling of democracy. The black slaves of America likewise needed this time of schooling because their various native African tribes had existed in a state of barbarism and savagery for thousands of years. To take a race of people from such a situation on one continent and transplant it to another with the full rights of equality that it took Anglo-Saxons hundreds of years to qualify for would not be wise. Blacks simply were not yet prepared for self-rule and independence as were white Americans, said the apologists.

In answer to the abolitionists' charges that slavery was contrary to the Declaration of Independence, the apologists pointed out that the Declaration was written by a southern slave holder, Thomas Jefferson. They asked, did Jefferson mean literally *all* men when he said that "all men are created equal," or did he really mean all *white* men? The answer was the latter, they said; it must have been because Jefferson did not free his slaves. They argued that it was axiomatic—that is to say, it was so clearly understood by everyone in the generation of the Founding Fathers that "all men" meant all white men that no one ever saw a need to express that thought openly in the Declaration of Independence.

Besides, said the apologists, the Declaration of Independence was not the law of the land. Yes, it established the United States on paper, but it had no authority in law. The law of the land, they said, was the Constitution, and it was quite different from the Declaration in its positions on the issue of slavery. The Constitution did allow slavery. It placed limitations on it, but it nevertheless allowed it. It, in fact, protected the right of slave holders to own slaves. Slaves were considered property according to the law, and no one could take away the property of an American citizen who obeyed the laws of the land and paid his taxes. The Constitution thus trumped the Declaration of Independence, and as far as the defenders of slavery were concerned, the legal case was closed.

On humanitarianism, according to the apologists, the average southern slave holder treated his slaves better than the average northern factory owner treated his white immigrant employees. The term "paternalism" (fatherliness) is often used to explain their position on this issue. They claimed that they treated their slaves like they treated their children. They fed them, clothed them, sheltered them, gave them medical care, and provided them with a sort of retirement system when they became too old and feeble to work. The northern factory owners could not say the same for their employees. All that factory workers got was a measly little paycheck, from which they had to pay their rent, buy their food and clothes, and provide for their own medical care (which they usually could not afford). And there was no retirement system for northern employees. When a worker grew too old and feeble to work, he was simply cast aside like yesterday's trash and replaced with a young, healthy worker. The same was true for workers who got injured on the job. There was no compensation for them. They were simply replaced with someone who could get the job done. All in all, said the apologists, the black slaves of the South were better off than free white northern factory workers.

On top of these arguments of religion and rationalism, the apologists added their socioeconomic theories. They said that slavery provided a necessary social control over a group of people that was not yet prepared for freedom. If the slaves were all suddenly set free, they said, there would be chaos. The black population of the South would either collectively starve to death because they did not have the know-how to provide for themselves within the white man's capitalist economic system or they would turn to theft and robbery or begging. Either way, no good could come from freeing the slaves. Besides, some blacks might want revenge against their old masters. There could be an incredible amount of violence and bloodshed and death resulting from the liberation of the slaves. Even worse, as they knew some white northerners would reckon it, thousands upon thousands of blacks might migrate northward to take up residence as their neighbors, as competitors for their jobs, and as suitors to their daughters. They questioned whether it would be worth the risk.

In addition to the need for social control of the large black population, the apologists claimed that they collectively had a personal investment in their slaves and in their cotton kingdom that was so great that the very economy of the United States depended upon it. Doing away with slavery, they said, would be tantamount to destroying the economic backbone of this country. The production of cotton would stop. White immigrants would not be willing and able to replace the slaves in the sweltering heat of the southern fields.

If the production of cotton stopped, a large part of the American shipping and trade industry would be adversely affected if not altogether ruined. The textile factories of the north would go out of business. Untold thousands of white northerners would be thrown out of work, the fortunes of northern investors would be destroyed, the tax base of governments at all levels would take a huge hit, and the nation's ability to pay its debts and keep healthy foreign relations would suffer. The nation could not adjust, evolve, and thus survive economically in light of such a scenario.

The apologists' fear of economic ruin proved partly true in the long run, at least for the South. A combination of factors caused it, including the destruction of infrastructure as a byproduct of war and the collective financial loss of billions invested in property in the form of slaves. The North's economy was not badly hurt even though about 80 percent of the nation's gross domestic product in 1860 was tied to slavery either directly or indirectly. The apologists' fear of a large free black population that was just as dependent on whites and the government after emancipation as during slavery also proved true in the long run, but the fear of violence and retribution did not. The notion that free blacks might overrun the North also proved partly true and partly false. In some cases, white southerners took great pains to prevent their leaving the South, lest they lose their labor force. Their self-congratulatory argument of paternalism omitted one monumentally important point: white northern factory workers had one thing that slaves did not have—freedom of choice about their employment, including where they worked, for whom they worked, and what job they held. Although all free workers' choices are always limited by unique individual circumstances as well as prevailing economic conditions nationally or globally, that is still better than having no choice at all.

The apologists' legal interpretation of the U.S. Constitution was like bedrock. The U.S. Supreme Court had always upheld the view that slaves were property and thus not subject to the rights afforded citizens, and it would continue to do so right up to the Civil War. This bedrock could not be penetrated by the sophistry of even the best legal minds; it could only be blasted by the dynamite of a constitutional amendment, as it finally would be in 1865. About their argument on the Declaration of Independence, as late as 1824, when the author

Thomas Jefferson was still alive, he had not disavowed their point of view, although he had also not cleared up what he meant, so it was mostly a moot point. Finally, their interpretation of the Bible required following the letter of the law rather than the general spirit or tenor of the scriptures. They seem to have been straining gnats while swallowing camels, so to speak, although there is room for reasonable people to disagree over that still today.

FOUR

Slavery, Abolition, and the West: 1848 to 1856

Manifest Destiny: The Mexican War and the Compromise of 1850

The abolition movement began as a religious phenomenon rather than a political one. Before the late 1830s, the slavery issue had intersected with national politics only sporadically. From about 1836 to 1846, it became the main political issue other than the Panic of 1837 for the presidents and Congress to deal with. By the late 1840s, it began to be essentially the only issue. Even though each administration from 1848 to 1865 tried to focus attention on other matters, ultimately the slavery question did not let them do it for long. Seemingly, every other issue that surfaced in the 1850s was tied either directly or indirectly to slavery. Because slavery became the great national political issue of the day, abolitionism found its loudest and most effective voice through politicians and statesmen at the time, not through preachers, professors, writers, or editors. Not surprisingly, therefore, the history of the abolition movement during these decades is devoted more to what happened on Capitol Hill and at the White House than on what happened in newspaper offices, pulpits, or the various antislavery societies' lecture circuits. People such as William Lloyd Garrison, Wendell Phillips, Frederick Douglass, and Abby Kelley Foster certainly made a lot of noise, but they simply could not make as much impact on history as their counterparts in Washington, D.C.

In the early 1840s, the United States already faced plenty of problems pertaining to slavery before the election of the proslavery southern Democrat James K. Polk to the presidency in 1844. Polk campaigned on annexing Texas and Oregon, which supporters believed were necessary steps in achieving America's "Manifest Destiny." The term implied that it was the will of God that the United States should spread its noble institutions—mainly democracy, Protestant Christianity, and slavery—across the North American continent. This religious belief and the political policy it produced threatened to put this country at odds with the nations claiming ownership of those territories, Mexico and Great Britain, respectively, a fact that Polk's opponents were quick to seize upon.

Henry Clay and the moderate Whigs saw the Democrat's position as arrogant, foolish, and dangerous because it amounted to saber-rattling with not one, but two, powerful nations at once. James G. Birney and the Liberty Party agreed but saw Texas and Oregon as separate issues. Whereas annexing Texas was all about guaranteeing the expansion of slavery to the West, annexing Oregon was not, at least not automatically or with certainty. The determination of Polk and the Democrats to force the issue in Texas was, therefore, merely one more manifestation of the slavocracy's wicked selfishness and callous disregard for the feelings of all antislavery Americans. William Lloyd Garrison and his nonpolitical abolitionists saw it as all that and more. To them, it was the final straw that should lead the righteous North to sever all ties with the evil South. "No Union with Slaveholders," which had been Garrison's motto for quite a while already, suddenly took on new meaning and urgency in 1844. It even resonated with some antislavery northern political leaders, such as John Quincy Adams, who had no affiliation with or appreciation for Garrison. Calls for the northern states to secede from the Union, unheard since the War of 1812, rang out again over the Texas issue.

Polk won the election because votes for Birney came at Clay's expense. The abolitionists had unintentionally helped the enemy they sought to destroy. Then, in another twist of fate, outgoing lame-duck President John Tyler signed the bill annexing Texas before Polk took office in 1845. Unfazed, Polk sent troops to the Texas–Mexican border and basically ensured and hastened a war with Mexico within a year. He chose to avoid war with Great Britain by negotiating a settlement for half of Oregon rather than demanding all of it. The Oregon problem was thus well on track to be resolved in 1846 when Mexico and the United States declared war on each other. The war proved quick and decisive in favor of the United States, resulting in the acquisition of a vast amount of territory in the West via the Treaty of Guadalupe-Hidalgo in 1848. This geographic aggrandizement, which added just as much land to the United States as that contained in the Louisiana Purchase or all the states east of the Mississippi River, was called the Mexican Cession. It included what later became the states of California, Nevada, and Utah, as well as most of Arizona and New Mexico and part of Texas, Oklahoma, Colorado, and Wyoming.

Near the beginning of the war, a Pennsylvania congressman named David Wilmot drew up a "Proviso" stipulating that slavery would not be permitted in any territory beyond Texas that the United States might acquire from Mexico. Submitting it as a rider (or earmark, in modern parlance) to a bill for funding military operations, the Wilmot Proviso enraged Polk's hawkish, proslavery supporters. The bill passed the House twice but was killed in the Senate both times. Sensing the futility of the situation, abolitionists from the Liberty Party began allying with northern Conscience Whigs and "Barn-burner" Democrats from New York for the first time, coalescing into a united antislavery front from 1846 to 1847. By 1848, they had formed a new and larger third party, which they called the Free Soil Party. Prominent founders included David Wilmot, Massachusetts Senator Charles Sumner, Ohio Congressman Joshua Giddings, and the old Liberty Party phalanx of Salmon P. Chase, Henry Stanton, and Joshua Leavitt. Holding a national convention in Buffalo, New York, they nominated Martin Van Buren for president and Charles Francis Adams for vice president. Their main plank was to prevent the expansion of slavery into the Mexican Cession, but they also addressed abolition by taking the gradualist rather than the immediatist position.

In the presidential election of 1848, the Free Soil Party garnered 291,000 popular votes, or five times more than the Liberty Party had received four years earlier. It was not nearly enough to win the White House. Free Soilers did manage to win 12 congressional seats, however, as well as controlling majorities in the Massachusetts and Ohio legislatures. Unfortunately for them, the Free Soil Party was essentially a one-issue party, and that issue, slavery's expansion into the Mexican Cession, would be settled in 1850, whereupon the party's main *raison d'etre* disappeared. Polk chose not to seek reelection in 1848, so the Democrats nominated Lewis Cass of Michigan. He had been one of the main proponents of the idea of giving each state or territory in the West "popular sovereignty," meaning the right to decide for itself whether it would allow slavery or not. This would mark a significant change from the procedure that had been in use since the era of the Articles of Confederation, when Congress began determining which new territories and states could have slavery and which could not.

The Whigs won the presidential election of 1848 by nominating the most prominent hero of the Mexican War, Zachary Taylor of Louisiana, for president, along with Millard Fillmore of New York for vice president. One was a proslavery southerner, the other a Doughface northerner, and that was perhaps the only winning formula the Whigs could have found at the time. Taylor had no prior political experience, and no one knew for sure what his views were on the most pressing issues of the day, but voters projected onto him that he had strong views on two key points: he was proslavery and pro-Union. These just happened to be the main issues of his brief administration, and they revolved around California and New Mexico—the only two areas of the Mexican Cession that had significant Anglo-American populations. Taylor encouraged the people of each area to forego forming a temporary territorial government and go ahead and draft state constitutions. He knew they would likely prohibit slavery in those constitutions, but at least it would prevent another ugly episode like the Texas problem.

Into this swirling mass of politics and racism was thrown the discovery of gold in California in 1849, which led to the most famous gold rush in American history. The swelling population and wealth of the San Francisco–Sacramento area led to the people of California following Taylor's advice, skipping a long phase as a legal territory and applying for admission to the Union as a free state immediately. This set off a crisis in which political leaders in several southern states, who got the nickname "Fire-Eaters," threatened secession should California be admitted. Meeting in Nashville, Tennessee, in 1850, the Nashville Convention, as it was called, brought the Union of states as close to a rupture as possible without one actually occurring. President Taylor responded to it in such a way as to leave no doubt that his loyalty to the Union was greater than his feelings about slavery, saying his fellow southerners must compromise on the issue or else face U.S. military force. He got his message out just in time; within a month, he was dead, and Millard Fillmore was sworn in as president.

Meanwhile, this California Crisis prompted the venerable old Henry Clay to try to come up with another compromise like the one he had helped push through Congress in the Missouri Controversy of 1820. He sponsored an omnibus bill that contained five proposals that pleased or offended one contingent of the American people or the other in just about equal proportions, whether pro- or antislavery. The five proposals in simplified form were (1) allow California to enter the Union as a free state; (2) give the rest of the Mexican Cession popular sovereignty; (3) abolish slave auctions in the nation's capital, Washington, D.C.; (4) reinforce and strengthen the Fugitive Slave Act; and (5) establish the still-disputed borders of Texas and have the U.S. government assume that state's war debts. Considering the divisiveness of these issues when taken separately, it is no wonder that debate over the omnibus bill was acrimonious. Clay could not get the bill passed on the first attempt. Being old, tired, and in poor health, he was forced to allow a younger man, Stephen A. Douglas, a Doughface Democrat from Illinois, to assume leadership of the bill.

A diminutive man, Douglas picked up the moniker "the little giant" for his ability to deftly maneuver his way through the nation's troubled political environment. Some observers called him "a steam engine in britches" for his work ethic and ability to get things done. He began his ascent to national prominence with his masterful work in guiding what came to be called the Compromise of 1850 to passage. He did it by breaking the omnibus bill into five separate bills and building bipartisan and bisectional coalitions to get each part passed in the Senate. That, plus the deaths of the three men who had been the most-influential politicians in the United States throughout the 1840s—the "Great Triumvirate" of Henry Clay, John C. Calhoun, and Daniel Webster—put Douglas in line to become the most powerful political figure in America in the 1850s. Inasmuch as he tied his political fortunes to the doctrine of popular sovereignty, however, his ascent and power would soon prove to be limited.

The Fugitive Slave Act and Uncle Tom's Cabin *Widen the North–South Divide*

President Fillmore signed the various parts of the Compromise of 1850 into law in September. All of the parts were controversial and divisive, but the one that caused the most antipathy by far was the new Fugitive Slave Act. Because several northern states had long resisted enforcing the old 1793 law, southerners demanded this stronger federal law to guarantee enforcement. The new law clarified the precise procedure to be used to catch fugitives, including what the duties of federal judges, U.S. marshals, and deputies were. It established a special office of commissioners that would organize manhunts and all the rest of the redention process. It specified that any law enforcement agent who refused to cooperate with the commissioners could be fined $1,000 and jailed for six months. It also prohibited fugitives from testifying in their own defense, counter-suing for freedom, or begging for mercy from the court.

As repulsive as he knew this law would be to most of his constituents, the venerable old statesman Daniel Webster made it the final cause of his Senate career to support passage of this bill. His ultimate goal was to preserve the Union at a time when it was by no means certain that the Union could be saved. He lived just long enough to see the backlash against the Fugitive Slave Act and to feel the wrath of his former supporters, who thought him a traitor.

Abolitionists considered this law the biggest outrage yet inflicted upon the nation by the slavocracy. It consequently turned more northerners into abolitionists than anything that had ever happened before. It also brought others who were already antislavery in sentiment out of the woodwork to be seen and heard for the first time. It converted the great Transcendentalist Ralph Waldo Emerson, for example, into an avowed abolitionist. It made his friend and fellow Transcendentalist Henry David Thoreau more outspoken and action oriented than he had ever been. It turned other Transcendentalists, such as Theodore Parker, Franklin Sanborn, and Thomas Wentworth Higginson, into absolute outlaws. But converts were not confined to the famous and influential of the population. Great and small alike began to join the cause, from the state legislatures to the street corner shops, from the farms to the cities, and from the churches to the saloons. It cut across all socioeconomic barriers. It prompted many southern free blacks to pack up and move north for safety, it led to the formation and reinvigoration of "vigilance committees" in various northern cities for preventing the enforcement of the law, and it provoked several northern state governments to pass new personal liberty laws that directly challenged federal authority.

The first test case of the new Fugitive Slave Law came in February 1851 in Boston when Frederick "Shadrach" Minkins, a Virginia slave, was captured and hauled to court. A team of abolitionist lawyers including Ellis Gray Loring and Samuel Sewall came to his defense. A group of local blacks and whites, led by Theodore Parker, calling themselves the Boston Vigilance Committee, burst into the courtroom, seized him, and hurried him to a safe but temporary hiding place. Minkins made it to Canada thereafter via the Underground Railroad, and his legal counselors were charged under federal law and prosecuted unsuccessfully by the Fillmore administration. Lewis Hayden, a Kentucky slave whose escape a few years earlier landed the Underground Railroad conductor Calvin Fairbank in prison for the next 13 years, played the key role in helping Minkins get to Canada.

A few other specific cases were noteworthy. Later in 1851, in the little town of Christiana, Pennsylvania, which is just north of the Mason–Dixon Line, the attempted arrest of four fugitive slaves by a group of slave catchers from Baltimore led to the owner and three black civilians being killed in a gunfight. The wrath of the federal government then fell upon the locals involved, as about 30 people were charged with treason, and some free blacks in the area were taken south and put into slavery.

In 1854, two important cases occurred. One was that of Anthony Burns, a Virginia slave who escaped to Boston and was arrested and thrown in jail. As happened in the earlier Shadrach Minkins case, the local Vigilance Committee sprang into action. Storming the courthouse, the abolitionists killed a U.S. law enforcement agent, but they were not able to break the heavily guarded prisoner free. His case thus went to court as scheduled, and his legal owner from Virginia was awarded custody. It took 2,000 federal troops and the Massachusetts militia, however, to guarantee his safe passage through town to the dock where a ship awaited that would take him back to slavery. He was carried through a gauntlet of some

50,000 angry Bostonians along the way. In the end, some of those same Bostonians purchased his freedom and brought him back.

In that same year, another fugitive case erupted when Joshua Glover, a slave from St. Louis, Missouri, escaped and was caught in Racine, Wisconsin. There he was thrown in jail to await a hearing. A group of local abolitionists broke into the jail and set him free. Authorities arrested a Milwaukee newspaper editor named Sherman Booth and sent him to trial in state court. His acquittal set off a chain of appeals and related suits, which culminated in the U.S. Supreme Court case *Ableman v. Booth*. It took years for the Roger B. Taney court to hear and make a ruling in the case, which resulted in a reversal of the lower court's decision and a conviction of Booth. By that time (1859), the ruling was anticlimactic because the Dred Scott case of 1857 had so shaken the nation that it did not seem to make much difference how the court ruled in *Ableman v. Booth*. Meanwhile, in 1856, one of the most bizarre and tragic cases in American history occurred in Cincinnati, Ohio. The focal point of the case was a slave mother of four from a farm in Boone County, Kentucky, named Margaret Garner, who fled across the river along with her husband and his parents to seek refuge with relatives in Cincinnati. She was 22 years old, and her children ranged from nine months to six years old. When a posse tracked down the fugitives, they surrounded the home and broke down the door. Garner just happened to be with one of her children, a two-year-old girl, at that moment. Garner cut the daughter's throat rather than allow her to be taken back into slavery. Two different legal suits arose from this event. The state of Ohio brought murder charges against her, but federal jurisdiction superseded what the state wanted. The fugitive slave suit was a federal case that seemed fairly clear; despite the fact that the defense attorney, John Jolliffe, argued that Garner had a compelling reason to run away—her white owner had raped her repeatedly and was the father of her children—the law said she must be returned. The whole family thus went back to Kentucky, whereupon the owner sold them all "down the river," as they said, to a plantation in Mississippi. Garner died there in 1858—ending one of the most truly sad and remarkable tales in the annals of slavery.

Even after the Civil War had started and raged on for two years, slave holders in the loyal border states (Delaware, Maryland,

Kentucky, and Missouri) continued to make claims for runaways under the 1850 law. Enforcement during wartime was quite obviously more difficult and was impossible in most cases. By the time the war ended and slavery was abolished, some 200 slaves had actually been captured and remanded to their southern owners. Clearly, the Fugitive Slave Law did not, as Henry Clay and Stephen A. Douglas had hoped, solve the problem of runaway slaves once and for all but rather generated catastrophic, unintended consequences.

While the new law was still in its infancy, other events transpired in the early 1850s that would greatly exacerbate sectional tensions. Among the most important of these was the publication of Harriet Beecher Stowe's monumental work of fiction, *Uncle Tom's Cabin*. Stowe was the daughter of Lyman Beecher, who had been the president of Lane Seminary in Cincinnati in 1834 when a conflict with the students led to their departure for Oberlin College (which then put Oberlin rather than Lane at the forefront of the abolition movement). While living with her father in Cincinnati, she had married one of Lane's professors, Calvin Stowe, with whom she had seven children. In 1850, the couple moved to Maine, where Calvin accepted a job teaching at Bowdoin College. Stowe was a well-educated woman interested in abolitionism, women's rights, education, and New England culture. Craving intellectual stimulation, self-fulfillment, and financial gain, she became a writer. She had already published a couple of books and several articles when she secured a job writing for a weekly periodical printed in Washington, D.C., by the American and Foreign Anti-Slavery Society called the *National Era*. The editor, Gamaliel Bailey, hired her to write a short story in a few installments that would personalize slavery for northern readers who had never had any real-life, personal interaction with slaves. Little did she or anyone else know how fortuitous this little job would be for either her career or the abolition movement as a whole.

The first installment appeared in June 1851. The story soon proved so popular, and the author became so enthralled in it, that Stowe eventually wrote 41 chapters, not bringing it to an end until April 1852. Subtitled *Life Among the Lowly*, this story of a black family's trials and tribulations in slavery succeeded at doing what Stowe and Bailey intended it to do—grip the heartstrings of readers to keep them coming back for more, and when possible, make converts to the abolition movement. With slight revisions, the complete story came out in book form later in 1852. Thousands who were not prone to picking up abolitionist papers such as the *National Era* read the book. Its impact was felt throughout the nation's capital and the northern states in a generally positive way, but its reception in the South was anything but positive.

Stowe's book was not the first work of fiction about American slavery ever published. In 1836, for example, Richard Hildreth had written *The Slave, or Memoirs of Archie Moore*. In 1851, just before Stowe started *Uncle Tom's Cabin*, Emily Catharine Pierson came out with *Jamie Parker, The Fugitive*. Neither book made an unusually great impact. *Uncle Tom's Cabin*, however, sold more than one million copies. It was the first American book to do so. It spawned imitators and proslavery rebuttals alike in just about equal proportions. Between 1852 and 1865, some 27 of the latter hit the market, mostly designed to refute the basic idea promulgated by Stowe of slavery's inherent evilness. They painted slavery in a favorable light and portrayed slaves as generally happy people. W. L. G. Smith's *Uncle Tom's Cabin As It Is; or, Life at the South* (1852) and Mary Eastman's *Aunt Phyllis's Cabin; or Southern Life As It Is* are exemplary of this literary fad. Such critics sniped at Stowe's work by saying that she was a Yankee who had never even stepped foot in the South and therefore did not have a clue what she was talking about. Stowe responded in 1853 with *The Making of Uncle Tom's Cabin*, which showed her sources of information for the book—mainly southern newspapers.

The 1850s thereafter became partly a time for rehashing the arguments made by each side in the 1830s and 1840s through slave narratives, religious tracts, and all kinds of pamphlets. However, there were a few original literary works put out at that time. George Fitzhugh of Virginia, for example, published *Sociology for the South* (1854) and *Cannibals All!* (1857), which articulated beliefs that many southerners already held about the inferiority of blacks and the need to keep them enslaved for their own good, and David Christy of Ohio published *Cotton in King* (1855), which set forth in final form the grand economic case for keeping slavery intact. On the abolitionists' side, the main intellectual advancement in the case against slavery came not from a northerner, oddly enough, but from a southerner named Hinton R. Helper of North Carolina. He argued against slavery based on its deleterious effects on his fellow poor southern whites in his 1857 book *The Impending Crisis of the South and How to Meet It*. To call Helper an abolitionist in the traditional sense of the word is to insult most other abolitionists, who had some semblance of racial equality and justice in their thinking about slaves and free blacks. Helper, by contrast, was a racist who cared nothing for the welfare of blacks but merely wanted to rid the nation of slavery to uplift poor whites and reform the South's one-dimensional economy. The case for Helper's anti-southern elitism was bolstered by the writings of a northern landscape architect, the very founder of systematic landscape architecture, named Frederick Law Olmsted. He criticized the South as culturally backward and aesthetically ugly compared with his New England homeland, saying essentially that slavery had a retarding influence on a majority of southerners—an extremely condescending thing to say.

Ripping Wide the Sectional Wound: Bleeding Kansas and Bleeding Sumner

At the time the presidential election of 1852 rolled around, Americans were thoroughly divided over slavery, and the two sides were never to be reconciled. The Whigs spurned incumbent President Millard Fillmore and nominated a Mexican War hero named Winfield Scott of Virginia, hoping to continue their formula for success that had won them the elections of 1840 and 1848. The Whigs ran an ineffective campaign, failing to distinguish themselves from the mostly proslavery Democrats by endorsing the Compromise of 1850 and the Fugitive Slave Law. The Free Soil Party, on its last leg, nominated John P. Hale of New Hampshire. Although Hale picked up more than 150,000 votes, that number barely dented the total of votes cast. The Democrats nominated Franklin Pierce, a Doughface from New Hampshire who had fought under Scott's command in the Mexican War. He was a compromise candidate who had never offended anyone in the party. Pierce and the Democrats walked away with the presidency.

Pierce's presidency would be short and full of trouble. It began even before Pierce was sworn in, with a train wreck that killed his

11-year-old son—the third of his three children to die. This tragic and untimely death caused Pierce and his first lady to enter the White House in grief and mourning. He was distraught and distracted and may have turned back to drinking, which he had given up earlier in life. To add insult to injury, his vice president, William R. King, died just one month after taking office, leaving his friend, confidant, and Secretary of War, Jefferson Davis of Mississippi, as the most powerful advisor in his administration. Davis's influence turned out to be not merely important but the defining characteristic of Pierce's term because it determined the direction of the administration in dealing with the West and with slavery.

The main issue facing the Pierce administration in 1853 was getting a transcontinental railroad built. Ever since the clarion calls for Manifest Destiny began to be heard in the 1840s, discussion of a railroad connecting the eastern United States with the West Coast could be heard in the background. When California, Oregon, and the rest of the newly acquired western territories were added to the United States, the talk of a transcontinental railroad increased and grew louder. Although virtually everyone agreed that such a transportation system was needed, the question that broke down agreement was that of precisely where to build this rail line. Everyone knew that this one-of-a-kind line would be a huge economic boon to whatever region of the country secured it, so both the North and the South wanted it badly. Exacerbating this problem was the fact that anywhere it was built within the current borders of the country from north to south would require crossing the Rocky Mountains. Engineering technology had not yet progressed to the point where it was a certainty that building over or through mountains on that scale was feasible.

Railroad engineers who had already been studying the problem for years knew the most suitable location for laying track was just below the current border with Mexico—the border just agreed upon in the 1848 Treaty of Guadalupe Hidalgo—which was south of the Gila River and the Arizona and New Mexico territories. This was propitious for Davis, a southerner, because he and all his fellow southern political leaders wanted this railroad to run to a southern city in the East, such as New Orleans, rather than a northern one such as Chicago. He wasted no time in persuading President Pierce to send diplomats to negotiate with Mexico for the purchase of that territory on behalf of a private American railroad firm. After protracted negotiations with Mexico and after yet more deal cutting in the U.S. Senate, the United States acquired a 30,000-square-mile tract of desert for $10 million. It became known as the Gadsden Purchase.

At the same time the Senate was finishing consideration of this deal in 1854, it was just beginning debate on the Kansas-Nebraska Bill, which would derail the whole transcontinental railroad debate. Douglas of Illinois had long wanted the transcontinental line to be built to Chicago, and he saw the Kansas-Nebraska Bill as his golden opportunity. The bill would organize Kansas and Nebraska into two new territories and soon-to-be free states, as the Missouri Compromise had specified more than three decades earlier. Douglas hoped to make a deal with southern senators that would potentially turn Kansas and Nebraska into slave states in exchange for the transcontinental railroad running to Chicago. Kansas and Nebraska would have popular sovereignty rather than requiring them by federal law to be free. After serious negotiations were concluded, the two sides agreed; the Missouri Compromise was repealed, and the people of each territory would decide for themselves whether to form free states or slave states. Both Secretary of War Davis and President Pierce approved the plan, although Pierce did so reluctantly.

Abolitionists in Congress did not approve the plan, but as usual, they were in the minority. Salmon P. Chase, Charles Sumner, Joshua Giddings, Geritt Smith, and others drew up a protest against it called "The Appeal of the Independent Democrats in Congress, to the People of the United States," stating their objections. They lost the debate, and the Kansas-Nebraska Act became law on May 30, 1854. In organizing for this battle, however, they formed the nucleus of a new national political party to replace the dying Whig Party, the decaying Free Soil Party, and the divided American or "Know-Nothing" Party. It would become known as the Republican Party, and its organization occurred at the state and local level in Wisconsin, Michigan, Iowa, and New Hampshire, while the debate in Washington was still ongoing.

Although it took a couple of years to coalesce, the Republican Party ultimately brought together all of the antislavery men from the North into one party, something that seems in hindsight to have been long overdue. It largely broke down the barriers between the abolitionist radicals (members of abolition societies and those who believed slavery was the great issue of the day to the exclusion of other issues) and the moderates (those who opposed slavery but did not necessarily consider it an exclusively important issue). It was devoted to three complementary things: free land, free labor, and free men. In retrospect, it is clear that from its inception, the days of slavery in America were numbered, although that certainly was not in evidence at that time. William Lloyd Garrison and his nonpolitical allies, for instance, continued to hold out, putting no faith in the party's ability to get slavery abolished. In illustration, Garrison himself, who had been denouncing the U.S. Constitution for a decade already by this time, now went so far as to burn it publicly in Framingham, Massachusetts and to stomp its ashes. He and his followers would eventually come around to support the party, at least marginally, but not until the middle of the Civil War.

Meanwhile, if ever there was a case where an arguably noble intention led to unintended consequences, it was the Kansas-Nebraska Act. Almost immediately in 1854–1855, proslavery Missourians who got the nickname "border ruffians" had begun to migrate directly next door into Kansas to vote in various local elections and to otherwise influence the outcomes by intimidating Free Soil voters. At the same time, abolitionists in New England, New York, and beyond began forming "Emigrant Aid" leagues and societies, whose function was to raise money, collect supplies, and send settlers to Kansas (to become something that might best be described as political missionaries) to offset the border ruffians. Some 1,300 of these abolitionist "emigrants" headed west over a matter of months. Henry Ward Beecher of Plymouth Congregational Church in Brooklyn, New York, who was the brother of Harriet Beecher Stowe and one of the best-known and most successful pastors in America, raised money to buy a shipment of Sharps .52 caliber rifles to send to Kansas. The rifles were packed into boxes marked "Bibles" to prevent federal or slave state officials from seizing them. "Beecher's Bibles," as they came to be known, were then used by the antislavery immigrants in Kansas to fight off the border ruffians.

One of the leaders of the Kansas Aid Society of Massachusetts was John Brown, who can only be described as the most radical of all radical abolitionists. He sent some of his sons ahead to Kansas, and he soon joined them with supplies and reinforcements. Calling himself "Captain" John Brown, he quickly developed a reputation as a strong leader in bloody clashes with border ruffians. Telegraph lines strung across more than half of the vast continent carried news of these events to the East Coast. Consequently, in May 1856, Brown, in Kansas, would become forever linked in history to men and events transpiring in the halls of Congress in Washington, D.C.

In the U.S. Senate, meanwhile, an ongoing debate about slavery and abolitionism in America was underway—not an unusual occurrence in the 1850s. In the midst of the debate came an unexpected turn of events, and truly one of the most bizarre stories in all of American history. South Carolina Senator Andrew Butler, who had worked closely with Stephen A. Douglas to author the Kansas-Nebraska Act, made a speech in which he proclaimed the greatness of the South's way of life, saying in essence that slavery helped make the South superior to the North's society and culture. Butler, an old man who was partially paralyzed from a stroke, which caused him to drool from one side of his mouth as he spoke, became the target of an unwise and unnecessary verbal attack by Massachusetts Senator Charles Sumner. The Republican and abolitionist Sumner, growing increasingly frustrated over events in the West, apparently felt pushed over the edge by Butler's oration. He responded to it in his "Crime Against Kansas" speech by mocking Butler's physical disability and saying in effect that the senator from South Carolina epitomized the South's culture and way of life—both were ugly and crippled.

This type of ad hominem attack violated the long tradition of genteel parliamentarianism in the U.S. Senate. More importantly, it offended southerners generally, but it understandably enraged Butler's family. Butler's health prevented him from making any forceful reaction, so his nephew, Preston Brooks of South Carolina, a congressman in the House of Representatives just across the hall from the Senate chamber, answered in his stead a couple of days later. Following the southern aristocratic tradition, he and some accomplices approached Sumner, who was seated at his desk in the Senate. He got Sumner's attention and stated his case against him briefly. Sumner, taken aback, refused to apologize. Brooks then flew into a rage and swatted him sharply over the head with his hardwood, gold-handled walking cane. Sumner tried to defend himself, but to little avail. As he fell to the floor, Brooks thrashed him again and again in a few short seconds, until he broke his cane, while his accomplices kept Sumner's would-be rescuers at bay. Sumner, bleeding and unconscious, was hurt badly enough that he left Washington and went home to Boston, where he spent the next three years recovering. Brooks was subsequently censured by the House of Representatives. He resigned his seat in protest. The voters of South Carolina, proud of the forceful action that he took in, as they saw it, setting an abolitionist straight, reelected him. Admirers from all over the South sent Brooks new walking canes, encouraging him to use theirs the next time he needed to teach an abolitionist a lesson.

The caning of Sumner was like manna from heaven for abolitionist writers and speakers. To them, it was evidence to illustrate how slave holding made southern men lawless, wicked, and lacking in self-control. It bolstered the case for waffling Whigs, Free Soilers, and other miscellaneous individuals with antislavery sympathies to join the brand new Republican Party because it seemed that the time for compromises was now over; the time for northerners to stand their ground once and for all was finally here. Yet before the ink was dry on the headlines that proclaimed the "Bleeding Sumner" episode, John Brown was springing into action in Kansas, staging the most notorious act of violence by an abolitionist that the nation had seen. The Pottawatomie Creek Massacre in May 1856, in which Brown and his gang murdered five proslavery men in cold blood, happened just three days after the caning of Charles Sumner in Washington, D.C. Although Brown had started his abolitionist career as a peaceful man, once blood was on his hands, he never considered any other means to end slavery in the United States than that. He soon left Kansas, heading back to New England to raise money, supplies, and recruits for future expeditions to the West.

FIVE

Toward the Civil War: Slavery Meets Its Doom, 1856 to 1865

Drawing the Line in the Sand: Dred Scott and John Brown

The new Republican Party was ready for its christening in 1856. Holding its national convention in Philadelphia, it nominated John C. Fremont, an eccentric man with an odd assortment of credentials. Born in Savannah, Georgia, and raised in Charleston, South Carolina, Fremont grew up around slaves and slave holders but developed strong feelings against slavery. A sort of jack-of-all-trades explorer and pioneer, he acquired the nickname "the Pathfinder." He had lived an interesting and rather exotic life before his presidential bid. He served in the U.S. army in California during the Mexican War, where he was court martialed for insubordination. Yet he appeared heroic to many observers, and he had name recognition that helped propel him to the top of the Republican ticket in 1856.

By this time, a new antislavery voice had risen above the din of the northern media in the form of Horace Greeley. Editor of the *New York Tribune* since 1841, Greeley had long been known as an abolitionist, but he became an elite leader of the movement in the mid-1850s through his editorials, his publication of various abolitionists' investigative reporting on the situation in the West and the South, and his own book *The History of the Struggle for Slavery Extension or Restriction in the United States*. He mirrored the general tenor of the times in the movement, growing increasingly angry and impatient over defeats of abolitionism at the hands of the southern slave power in Washington, D.C. In some cases, he led the abolitionist masses, and in other cases, he followed the lead of the masses, but either way he became more prominent than other editors of note, such as William Lloyd Garrison. Part of his success lay in recognizing talent and putting it to work for him. He employed antislavery writers who would go on to distinguish themselves in letters, politics, business, and a variety of professions. They included Josiah Grinnell, Sydney Howard Gay, Carl Schurz, John Hay, Charles Dana, and William Dean Howells, just to name some. After Greeley's celebrity status was evident, his star continued to rise until, by 1872, he ultimately became a presidential candidate himself. In the meantime, however, he threw his support behind the new Republican Party, which reinforced its credibility.

In the election of 1856, the Democrats spurned Franklin Pierce and ran a career politician named James Buchanan of Pennsylvania for president, who, just like Pierce, was a northern Doughface. He believed that popular sovereignty was the best policy to pursue in the West. He had enjoyed a great amount of success as a diplomat and statesman before this time. However, he proved to be the wrong man to lead the nation through the troubled four years that lay ahead. Voters chose him over Fremont. Despite losing, Fremont and his new party had made an impressive first showing with nearly 1.4 million votes to Buchanan's 1.9 million while carrying 11 northern states. It was the closest an abolitionist had yet come to winning the White House.

Buchanan's presidency hardly could have begun worse. On the day of his inauguration, the U.S. Supreme Court informed him of their decision in what would quickly become the most important case in the history of American slavery, *Scott v. Sandford.* The case involved a slave named Dred Scott, who had lived much of his adult life as the personal servant of a U.S. army surgeon named Emerson, whose regular residence was in Missouri. In the 1830s, the army had required Emerson to move across the Mississippi River into the free state of Illinois and the free territories of Wisconsin and Minnesota. He took Dred Scott with him. Thus, the slave had lived on free soil for a few years, all the while remaining legally bound to his master. When Emerson died, his slave, through a complicated series of events, ended up in the possession of an abolitionist named John Sanford of New York. Although Scott could have been set free and spared years of personal misery, Sanford and his team of abolitionist lawyers, congressmen, and editors chose to use to him as something akin to a legal guinea pig, with the object being to try to gain liberty for all slaves who had ever been taken to live on free soil. (Based on the ruling in a similar case in Massachusetts in 1836 called *Commonwealth v. Aves,* there was a precedent for freeing slaves when they were taken to reside in a free state.) The plan required that Scott sue for his freedom. Thus, the Dred Scott case, as it was popularly known, wound its way through state and federal courts from 1846 to 1857 before the U.S. Supreme Court finally resolved it once and for all.

The U.S. Supreme Court at the time was composed of five proslavery justices, including Chief Justice Roger B. Taney of Maryland, and four antislavery justices. Not surprisingly, the ruling that Taney issued was not favorable to Scott. Reading the U.S. Constitution strictly, the court held that slaves were not citizens of the United States and therefore had no legal right to sue in federal court; the case must be thrown out. Not content merely to make this simple ruling, Taney took the opportunity to try to settle the whole issue of the extension of slavery into the West for all time and in so doing send a strong message to the abolitionists. Here an attempt to simplify and interpret what was a complex set of opinions and statements is in order. Basically, the court declared all federal laws that limited or prohibited slavery based on geographic lines unconstitutional. In that mix lay notably the old Missouri Compromise's 36–30 line, which had recently been uprooted by the Kansas-Nebraska Act. However, the Kansas-Nebraska Act itself, plus parts of the Compromise of 1850, were unconstitutional because they too allowed for slavery to exist only regionally, not nationally. The Taney court held that slavery should be legal throughout the nation because slaves were treated as property in the U.S. Constitution. Because the Constitution placed no restrictions on where a citizen could own any other type of property, such as a home, a horse, or a business, it likewise could not be construed to place restrictions on where a citizen could own this particular type of property (a slave). The bottom line here was that the court intended to have Congress go back to the drawing board in making laws on slavery and open all western territories and states to it.

Through a cold, rational reading of the U.S. Constitution, it can be argued that the court had made a ruling and offered an opinion that was technically accurate. It is certain, however, that if the court got the letter of the law right, it got the spirit of the law entirely wrong. Clearly, the Founding Fathers never intended that slaves be lumped together with horses and cattle despite all the vagaries they managed to write into the Constitution on the subject of slavery. Abolitionists uniformly denounced the Dred Scott decision as a miscarriage of justice at least as intolerable as the Fugitive Slave Act. The result was that, similar to each of the controversial events discussed herein that came before it in the 1850s, this decision swelled the ranks of the abolitionists even more. Now it likewise grew the young Republican Party.

The years of the Buchanan administration look in retrospect like a whirlwind of negative events that could have only one outcome: civil war. After all, the Garrisonians had been trumpeting their "No Union with Slaveholders" mantra for more than a decade, talk of northern state secession and war was now being heard from otherwise respectable leaders of the Republican Party such as William Seward of New York, the killing in Kansas continued, and John Brown was running to and fro making preparations for what would become the final straw leading to the "irrepressible conflict." In Kansas, proslavery settlers and free soil settlers each held separate constitutional conventions and produced opposing constitutions. Buchanan, after pledging to let popular sovereignty take its course in Kansas, reneged and threw his support behind the proslavery LeCompton Constitution, which abolitionists considered fraudulent. Even Stephen A. Douglas, who had written the law creating the conditions that made this fiasco possible, could not support Buchanan's position on this issue. The two leading Democrats in the nation were thus divided over the most important issue of the day, and the party would not recover from it in the next presidential election.

In the midst of all this commotion, the state of Illinois hosted a campaign between the incumbent Democrat Stephen A. Douglas and his Republican challenger, Abraham Lincoln, for a seat in the U.S. Senate. Lincoln had seemingly come out of nowhere to become a serious contender. Born in Kentucky and having seen slavery up close and personal, he grew up and became a country lawyer living in a free state in the West. Identifying with the Whigs in his early political career, he had served eight years in the Illinois legislature and one term in Congress, during which he opposed the Mexican War. As a legislator, he had a record of opposing the extension of slavery, but as a lawyer, he had represented both slave holders and antislavery clients alike. When Lincoln challenged Douglas to a series of debates in 1858, Douglas put him on the defensive about his racial views, forcing him to make it abundantly clear that he was not in favor of racial equality. It is tempting when reading Lincoln's statements on race in history to call him hypocritical on the issue, as could be said about Thomas Jefferson and several other great Americans from earlier generations, but a more accurate description of his views would perhaps be to call them complex and nuanced. He tried to walk the middle path on slavery and racial issues, where he believed a majority of his constituents in Illinois (and later most other northern states) stood. He certainly never called himself an abolitionist, which is ironic because he ultimately became the "Great Emancipator."

The main issue in question in the Lincoln–Douglas debates was the possibility of slavery's being introduced into all western territories as a result of the Dred Scott decision. Lincoln scored points with public opinion by blaming Douglas and his Kansas-Nebraska Act and its popular sovereignty plan for the Supreme Court's controversial ruling. Douglas scored points in return by accusing Lincoln of favoring abolition and racial equality, which forced Lincoln to defend himself against those unpopular positions. In the second debate, held at the town of Freeport, Illinois, Douglas calmed fears that popular sovereignty was now defunct as a result of the Dred Scott decision by arguing that slavery would not take root in any western territory or state unless the legislature there passed laws that were friendly to the institution. Therefore, even if the Supreme Court said that slavery could not be excluded from the territories, slave holders would be reticent to take slaves there if there were no adequate local legal protection and law enforcement for their "property." This argument came to be known as the Freeport Doctrine, and it was good enough to get Douglas reelected. Although Lincoln lost the race, he made a name for himself as a skillful debater and a first-rate articulator of Republican principles. Moreover, Lincoln's notoriety spread beyond the state of Illinois because the debates were publicized throughout the country. Lincoln thus became a national figure who would be tapped by the Republican Party in 1860 as its presidential nominee.

While the nation's attention in the mid-1850s was mainly focused on the events already discussed that emanated from Washington, D.C., and Kansas, behind the scenes and unknown to the American public, John Brown stayed busy plotting his great slave rebellion. In his efforts to recruit supporters, he made acquaintances with several men of standing and influence in the Northeast who came to be known as the "Secret Six." They included the wealthy Gerrit Smith of New York, a long-time political abolitionist who most recently had carried the mantle as the Liberty League's presidential nominee in 1856 and would do so again in 1860; George Luther Stearns, a wealthy Boston businessman who had funded the Emigrant Aid movement; Theodore Parker and Thomas Wentworth Higginson of Massachusetts, both Transcendentalist ministers who had been leaders of the Boston Vigilance Committee; Samuel Gridley Howe, a Boston physician who did pioneering work with blind people, was the husband of Julia Ward Howe and an important Underground Railroad operative; and Franklin B. Sanborn, a young Harvard graduate who would later distinguish himself as a writer and educator.

Among Brown's other backers were the loudest abolitionist voice in America, Wendell Phillips; the most prominent pastor in America, Henry Ward Beecher of New York; William Whitting, a wealthy Massachusetts businessman; Richard Realff, a British immigrant whom he met in Kansas; Harriet Tubman and Lewis Hayden, escaped slaves who became notable Underground Railroad operators; Josiah Bushnell Grinnell, one of the founding fathers of Iowa; Allan Pinkerton of Chicago, who would soon become famous as head of the Pinkerton Detective Agency that bore his name; and dozens of other people of wealth and influence. Brown had also met with Frederick Douglass, who supported his idea of starting a slave rebellion but opposed the specifics of his plan. William Lloyd Garrison, a determined pacifist, steadfastly refused to support anyone like Brown who advocated violence. Horace Greeley, another pacifist, did not support Brown either, but he published a letter in his *New York Tribune* that "the Captain" had sent him after his most recent activities in Missouri trying to justify his actions, which made him suspect as a secret supporter. Some of the aforementioned knew exactly what Brown's plan was, but others knew only generalities of his intentions.

After traversing half of the North American continent several times, engaging in a variety of abolitionist activities that included recruiting Christian "soldiers" and killing slave holders, Brown was finally ready in October 1859 to execute his grand plan. He chose the town of Harpers Ferry, Virginia (now West Virginia), the site of a U.S. Army weapons manufacturing and storage facility. It was also a town with few black residents and almost no slaves. His plan went horribly awry quickly, leaving him and most of his men in a predicament that would end poorly. Captured by U.S. military authorities the next day, Brown and five accomplices had seen 10 of their fellows killed, with only five escaping.

News of Brown's "raid" on Harpers Ferry spread like wildfire throughout the country and abroad. It was the most sensational event yet in this whole long, ugly saga. It was also the final straw in the minds of many southerners. It became for them what the beating of Sumner had been to abolitionists in 1856—a rallying cry of unity for all proslavery Americans. Almost immediately upon capture, Brown was interrogated by the governor of Virginia, a U.S. Senator, a congressman, and others. He was then summarily tried, convicted, sentenced, and hanged within barely more than a month. Justice in this case was meted out by the state of Virginia rather than the United States government, with the blessing of President Buchanan. Six co-conspirators were executed over the next three months. Towns all across the South, not knowing whether Brown's raid was a one-time occurrence or whether there would be others like it, began gearing up for battle, both mentally and physically.

Some of Brown's supporters and acquaintances, including all of the Secret Six except for Higginson, fled the country or went into hiding in fear of being implicated as conspirators in his crimes. Others who had been less conspicuously attached to him, such as Henry Ward Beecher, Henry David Thoreau, Ralph Waldo Emerson, Lydia Maria Child, and Julia Ward Howe, came out of the woodwork to laud him as a hero. Some abolitionists who had no connection to Brown at all, such as John G. Fee and Cassius Clay of Kentucky, were attacked physically or verbally by proslavery mobs. Republican political leaders such as Benjamin Wade of Ohio and hopefuls such as Abraham Lincoln of Illinois quickly tried to distance themselves from Brown, assuring voters that this self-styled "Captain" was a madman and that the party did not even remotely share his views or approve his actions. William Seward, the leading Republican in New York, failed to distance himself from Brown vigorously and persuasively enough and thus saw his presidential hopes dashed the following year. Efforts by proslavery and Doughface editors to link Brown to Horace Greeley made great fodder for the newspapers but ultimately failed for lack of evidence, and Greeley and his paper survived intact.

Drawing the Battle Lines: The Election of Lincoln and the Coming of the Civil War

At the same time as the raid on Harpers Ferry, the presidential hopeful Lincoln accepted an invitation to speak at Henry Ward Beecher's church in Brooklyn, New York. He delivered this speech, which became the most important of his political career thus far, in February 1860, not at Beecher's Plymouth Church but at Cooper Union hall in Manhattan. Continuing to tread the middle ground between opposition to the expansion of slavery and the fanaticism of abolitionists such as John Brown, Lincoln laid out a legal case that would impress any lawyer but that could be understood by the average American as well. Horace Greeley and other influential New York Republicans took notice, and the speech helped clear his path to the nomination.

This was much to the consternation of radicals such as William Lloyd Garrison and Wendell Phillips, who by this time had gathered more momentum than ever for their cause of disunion. Notable Garrisonians who supported northern state secession included Parker Pillsbury, Elizur Wright, Thomas Wentworth Higginson, Stephen Foster, and Samuel J. May, among others. They had little confidence in the Republican Party and even less in Lincoln, in light of his many public concessions to the slave power. It seemingly did not matter anyway. Considering that the Republican Party was barely five years old and that this would be only its second presidential race, the odds of Lincoln's winning seemed remote—at least barring some kind of implosion by the Democrats.

Implode is just what the Democrat Party did. Divided over what course to take on the all-important issue of the expansion of slavery to the West, the party split at its national convention in Charleston in April 1860. Northern Democrats chose Stephen A. Douglas as their nominee, holding fast to the controversial doctrine of popular sovereignty. The Fire-Eater faction of southerners walked out in disgust; they demanded a stronger platform than popular sovereignty. They wanted to force slavery on the territories in the West. The party thus called another convention to be held in Baltimore in June. There the voting turned out the same except that the Fire-Eaters grew in number. This time when they walked out, they decided to hold their own separate convention in Richmond and nominate their own candidate. Their nominee, John C. Breckinridge of Kentucky was the current vice president for James Buchanan. Thus, the Democrats fielded two candidates in the election of 1860 and in so doing sealed their doom and Lincoln's victory.

There was also a fourth party vying for votes, the Constitutional Union Party, which chose John Bell of Tennessee as its nominee. This small party was composed of former Whigs and Know-Nothings who cared little one way or the other about the slavery issue but instead wanted to keep the Union together under the current Constitution at any cost. Under the circumstances, this party actually had the most rational platform of any in the field in 1860. It was destined to get little support in the North and barely more in the Deep South. It did make a showing in the border states, but it was not enough.

Many, perhaps most, white southerners in 1860 were under the impression that the Republican Party was the political wing of the abolition movement. Many Republicans were indeed abolitionists, but many were not. Lincoln himself clearly was not. He was instead representative of a sizeable number of Republicans who merely wanted to check the spread of slavery and the growth of the institution. It scarcely mattered to the average southern voter. The Fire-Eaters had been issuing philippics against antislavery politicians for years, and Lincoln was undoubtedly an antislavery man. This group of proslavery radicals, which included J. D. B. DeBow of Louisiana, Robert Rhett of South Carolina, Edmund Ruffin of Virginia, and William Lowndes Yancy of Alabama, among others, was getting larger and more influential by the day in 1860. They warned all who would listen that they were ready to lead their states to secede if Lincoln were to win election. It was not an idle threat. Nor was the saber rattling that accompanied their secession speeches and writings merely insincere noise. They threw down the gauntlet, and it had come to this: the Fire-Eaters were ready to go to war to preserve their freedom to keep others enslaved, and they had persuaded a majority of their fellow southerners to agree with them. When Lincoln won the election, with only 39 percent of the popular vote but a sizeable majority of the electoral college vote, the conditions were set for secession and war.

Although all aspects of the Lincoln administration are historically important, only the aspects that touched upon the freeing of the slaves are crucial here. Therefore, a narrowly focused discussion of Lincoln and the Civil War in relation to abolitionism follows. First, after the November election, Senator John J. Crittenden of Kentucky tried to stop the movement for southern secession through offering a series of compromises in the tradition of deceased fellow Kentuckian Henry Clay. Similar to the Constitutional Union Party, however, the "Crittenden Compromise," as the bundle of trade-offs was called, had few supporters among the polarized sections and parties. Lincoln and the Republican Party rejected it; the Fire-Eaters ignored it and carried out their threat, leading seven southern states in rapid succession to leave the Union from December 1860 to February 1861.

Even then, some political leaders in Washington, D.C., clung to hope that the Union could be restored. Thomas Corwin, a Republican congressman from Ohio, offered a constitutional amendment in March 1861 which would have guaranteed that the U.S. government would never abolish slavery in the states where it already existed. It passed both the House of Representatives and the Senate and was tacitly approved by President Lincoln. It was sent to the various states for ratification. Ohio, Maryland, and Illinois ratified it. By that time, however, shots had been fired, the war had begun, more southern states had seceded, the Confederate States of America had been formed, and the time for compromise had passed. Other states thus never got around to ratifying it. The irony of the Corwin amendment is that it would have been the 13th Amendment to the U.S. Constitution. Instead, the 13th Amendment that was finally passed and ratified four years later would be the one that abolished slavery throughout the nation.

The first year of the war was not good for the Union, the North, the Republican Party, the Lincoln administration, or the abolition movement. The South won most of the battles, Lincoln was excoriated in the press as an incompetent leader, and freedom for the slaves seemed further away than ever. Yet, one interesting turn of events in that terrible year was that radical abolitionists such as William Lloyd Garrison saw the proverbial light and decided to throw their support behind Lincoln and the Union war effort. Now that southerners had beaten him to the punch of secession, Garrison's disunionism had become an untenable position. They had little if anything to lose by changing courses at this point and potentially much to gain by pressuring the Lincoln administration to free the slaves. Thus, in 1861, a group of Boston abolitionists led by Samuel Gridley Howe, Franklin Sanborn, and Moncure Conway formed the Emancipation League for that purpose.

Meanwhile, both Garrison and Phillips seized the opportunity to revisit the lecture circuit and stir up northern public sentiment. At this time, it became evident that Garrison, the great founding father of the abolition movement, had seen his better days. Phillips, younger and considerably more vigorous, was a much more effective speaker, and he attracted audiences of thousands. His message was simple and forceful: free the slaves now, destroy the southern army and government, and give back to the white people of the South what they had been giving to blacks for decades. The war was rapidly making South haters out of many moderate northerners, so Phillips's message resonated with them. Horace Greeley echoed that message from the *New York Tribune,* and abolitionists in Congress, such as Charles Sumner, Thaddeus Stevens, and Henry Wilson, repeated it from Capitol Hill.

Lincoln was impervious to such pressure in 1861. When Union general Benjamin F. Butler seized a group of slaves and gave them quasi-freedom, while putting them to work for the U.S. army, Lincoln rebuffed him and later fired him. Congress, however, thought Butler closer to having the right idea than the president about seizing the human "property" of slave holders and calling them "contraband of war." It passed a Confiscation Act to that end. Lincoln yielded to

Congress on this point but then rescinded General John C. Fremont's proclamation freeing slaves of Confederates and their sympathizers in Missouri shortly thereafter. Lincoln's policies could, again, look hypocritical or wishy-washy on the surface, but his stance was actually very nuanced, as his lawyer's mind made important distinctions on subtle points about freeing slaves under certain circumstances but not others.

In early 1862, various groups of abolitionists traveled to Washington to get an audience with the president to lobby for immediate emancipation. Some were successful at least at getting the audience, including those led by Wendell Phillips and Oliver Johnson. Lincoln listened and pondered their opinions, but he still had his own, and he was not ready to abandon his middle-of-the-road position just yet. The situation on the battlefields had not improved, however, by the summer of 1862, and he was getting desperate. When he and the Republican-controlled government passed the Militia Act in 1862, allowing for the recruitment of black soldiers into the U.S. army, abolitionists were heartened. A second Confiscation Act, designed to clarify the government's policy on slaves who were liberated or otherwise aided as an unavoidable consequence of war, actually made the policy more unclear than before. Nonetheless, these were important steps. The next few steps would come rapidly as exigencies of the war, and Lincoln's position on freeing the slaves would get pushed to the forefront of his overall war strategy rather than remaining an unwanted complication to waging the war. Lincoln would be pushed further than he perhaps wanted to go and faster than he wanted to get there, but he was inching in the direction of emancipation in his own mind regardless.

In September 1862, after the pivotal Battle of Antietam Creek in Maryland, Lincoln notified the nation of his decision to free the slaves in the southern states that were at war with the United States but not in the loyal border states of Maryland, Delaware, Kentucky, and Missouri. The policy was to take effect on January 1, 1863, and would be called the Emancipation Proclamation. On the one hand, it appeared to be yet another case where Lincoln was a little too fond of the middle path, but on the other hand, it was potentially a brilliant political maneuver. The obvious question was whether it made sense to proclaim slaves free in states where currently Lincoln had no way to enforce the proclamation and leave them in bondage in states where he actually had the power to liberate them. The answer was that two positive things might be accomplished and two negative things avoided. One negative thing that Lincoln hoped to avoid was alienating more white people in the loyal border states. Freeing the slaves there could cause an economic and social upheaval that might impel a majority to choose secession and join the Confederacy.

Another negative thing that Lincoln hoped to prevent was England and France's allying with the Confederacy. Those two leading industrial nations depended on southern-grown cotton for their economies to function at peak level. Disruption in the cotton supply because of the war had been threatening to draw either or both nations in on the side of the Confederacy from the beginning. Yet neither nation really wanted to help the Confederacy because both had already abolished slavery in their own realms and thus did not want to lend outright moral support or military aid to that institution, although both had done so indirectly for decades by buying cotton from the American South.

The first positive thing that Lincoln hoped to achieve was to incite some slaves to rise up and claim their freedom by walking off the job, running away, or otherwise refusing to stay in their positions of servitude. Just to know that the U.S. government had declared them free could give them the impetus to do what perhaps had been in their power all along but they had been afraid to do. Another positive thing, which was tied to this second factor, that Lincoln hoped to accomplish was to force slave holders—many of whom were also officers in the Confederate Army—to worry more than usual about slave uprisings back home while they were off fighting the war. Whether their slaves actually rebelled or ran away, they would be distracted by that possibility and hence not be as effective on the battlefield. It could even lead some to abandon their posts and go home to manage their domestic affairs.

Thus, the Emancipation Proclamation was an important piece of wartime propaganda. Although it may not have freed the slaves in an immediate, physical, technical sense, it offered freedom psychologically, and it put the U.S. government on record as opposing slavery in a direct and forceful way for the first time. Once on record, the nation could scarcely renege on that position in years to come, regardless of the outcome of the war. Thereafter, as the war dragged on into the summer of 1863, the tide swung in favor of the Union with major victories at Vicksburg and Gettysburg. Abolitionists could now see the light at the end of the tunnel. In 1863, several resolutions were introduced in the House of Representatives to abolish slavery throughout the United States, including one by Owen Lovejoy, an Illinois congressman and younger brother of Elijah Lovejoy, who had been martyred back in 1837. The House initially voted down the resolutions, but the Senate approved a universal emancipation resolution in April 1864. The House followed suit in January 1865. At that point, the 13th Amendment to the United States Constitution was proposed and sent to the 36 states for ratification.

Meanwhile, as the war was grinding to a close in the spring of 1865, Lincoln was sworn in for his second term, the various states began voting on the 13th Amendment one by one, and Congress created a new federal agency called the Bureau of Refugees, Freedmen and Abandoned Lands (popularly known as the Freedmen's Bureau) to provide relief for the displaced millions of black southerners. By mid-April, the war was essentially over, Lincoln was dead, and almost all of the slaves had claimed their freedom, although some slaves in remote areas such as Texas did not get the news until later in the summer. By December 1865, two-thirds of the states had ratified the 13th Amendment, and slavery in the United States was no more. More than 3.9 million slaves—the former property of some 394,000 slave holders—were now free human beings under the law. What happened next is called Reconstruction, and it is a whole other story.

Post-Abolitionism, Racial Equality, and the Historiography of the Abolition Movement

Upon ratification of the 13th Amendment, there could be no more abolitionism in the United States, so there was no further need for abolitionists or antislavery societies. William Lloyd Garrison decided that his life's work was done. He published the last edition of the *Liberator* in December 1865. He could now retire and live out the rest of his days knowing he had triumphed in one of the epic battles in all of history. He could thus die a happy man, although he would live for several more years before he did. He was destined to go down in history as the single most important of all abolitionists, despite that fact that, after the schism of 1840, he and his organization sank into the background of public attention. Partly this is because Garrison was the chief founding father of the movement, and partly it is because Garrison's legacy as an egalitarian extraordinaire has been bolstered by the success of the women's rights movement in more recent times. Finally, partly it is because of Garrison's support for and connection with Frederick Douglass, who came to be the most important African American of the nineteenth century and who has become one of the great heroes of black history since the civil rights movement of the 1960s.

Other abolitionists were not ready to end their life's work at that time, however. They were ready to transform it instead. Their new goal was to ensure civil rights and racial equality for the former slaves. Wendell Phillips enjoyed several years as the premier white representative of this group, at least among those who were not political officials, and Frederick Douglass became the leading black spokesman for racial equality. But the political officials were the ones in the spotlight. Charles Sumner, Benjamin F. Wade, and Henry Wilson were among the leading spokesmen in the U.S. Senate, and Thaddeus Stevens, George W. Julian, and Josiah Grinnell ranked among the same in the House of Representatives. These aforementioned congressmen and senators had many allies on Capitol Hill— all Republicans—who collectively were willing and able to pass laws and make policies designed to help the former slaves. Some former abolitionists-turned-civil rights advocates enjoyed long careers during Reconstruction and beyond. Some got entangled in political and financial corruption that ended their careers, and others were replaced in regular elections by constituents who did not appreciate the continued focus on racial issues. Some died before they had to worry about reelection or retirement.

The years 1865 through 1868 proved hard for the former slaves. President Andrew Johnson, a southern Democrat who took over upon the death of Lincoln, had opposed slavery and approved of emancipation but thereafter showed little concern for the welfare of the free black population. Constitutionally conservative, he conflicted with the "big government" Republicans who controlled Congress and who sat in the Cabinet he inherited from Lincoln. Notably, he opposed the 14th Amendment that made blacks U.S. citizens and the Civil Rights

Act of 1866 that gave them the same legal rights that whites enjoyed. Ultimately, the two sides would clash in an ugly impeachment episode over these issues (although Republicans cited technical, legal reasons for the impeachment). Meanwhile, the southern states attempted to handle their free black populations in their own ways, which were totally different from the northern Republican vision for a postslavery nation. The result was a clash between the states and the federal government that resulted in the creation and dissolution of the Ku Klux Klan and military occupation of the South. In 1869, the situation took an apparent major turn for the better when the northern Republican Ulysses S. Grant was elected president. Much friendlier toward blacks, he worked with Congress rather than against it to ensure that the 14th Amendment was enforced and the 15th Amendment guaranteeing black voting rights was passed and enforced. Matters worsened rapidly after the presidential election of 1872 because Grant's presidency was tainted by scandals and corruption that caused Congress to go Democrat for the first time since before the Civil War and left the former slaves without an effective advocate in the White House or on Capitol Hill. Pressed hard by Democrats, southerners, and constitutional conservatives of other types, Grant and his successor Rutherford B. Hayes were painted into a corner where they had little choice but to end the Reconstruction experiment in racial equality. The former slaves were thus left to fend for themselves in a nation that was overwhelmingly hostile to them as of 1877. The former abolitionists could do nothing about it. Their complaints fell on deaf ears.

In evaluating the abolitionists and their movement as a historical phenomenon, historians have not always reached a uniform conclusion. The differing evaluations have been caused by three main factors: political partisanship, racial views, and generational revisionism. At the end of the Civil War and throughout Reconstruction, the prevailing point of view about abolitionism was written by the abolitionists themselves and was, not surprisingly, positive. In the Gilded Age and early years of the twentieth century that followed, conservative historians who were sympathetic to the white South and racist in their worldview took preeminence. Some of them had lived through the Civil War and Reconstruction and remembered it as a bad time, and others had heard stories from their elders that personalized those years for them in a negative way. They were consequently critical in their views of the abolitionists. In the mid-twentieth century, as the civil rights movement began to gear up, a new generation arose that neither remembered that part of the American past from personal experience nor had many elders around them who did. They were mostly in favor of civil rights reforms in their own time, and they reevaluated the abolitionists in a positive light as having been their nineteenth-century counterparts— they were humanitarians, sociopolitical reformers, and indeed world changers. In the late-twentieth and early twenty-first centuries, the general trend is still to see the abolitionists overall in a positive light, but more emphasis is now put on the role of blacks themselves in achieving freedom than upon their white allies. The same can be said of the role of women in the movement. Although the first abolitionists were men, one can only wonder whether the movement would have ultimately succeeded had there been no great inclusion of female participants. Modern scholarship has placed more emphasis on women's contributions. Another recent trend has been to deemphasize the role of Christianity in the abolition movement. However, there would have been no abolition movement without there first being a large group of determined evangelical Christians who were willing to stick their necks on the proverbial chopping block for this unpopular issue.

Biographical Profiles of
Key Abolitionists

Benjamin Lundy (1789–1839)

The first to make a name for himself nationally as a full-time abolitionist, Lundy was born on January 4, 1789, to a Quaker family in New Jersey. He grew up in an environment that cultivated antislavery sentiment, and it profoundly affected him. As an adult, he moved west to Wheeling, Virginia (today West Virginia), a city on the Ohio River, where he apprenticed as a saddle maker and came into contact with slaves and slavery in person for the first time. Soon thereafter, he moved across the river to Ohio, where he began to encounter operatives on the Underground Railroad, got married, and started a family and a business. At Saint Clairsville, in 1816, he formed an abolitionist organization called the Union Humane Society. Thus began his antislavery activism.

In 1817, Lundy moved to Mount Pleasant, Ohio, and started writing articles for the *Philanthropist,* a paper founded by Charles Osborne, which is generally held to be the first real abolitionist newspaper in American history. The Missouri Controversy was erupting at the time, however, and Lundy saw a golden opportunity to make an impact on the slavery question in the American West. Moving to St. Louis, he began to crusade against Missouri's admission to the Union as a slave state. Although unsuccessful, he gained valuable experience, which he took back to Ohio with him and used in his next venture.

In Mount Pleasant again, in 1821, Lundy published the inaugural issue of the *Genius of Universal Emancipation,* which was the first abolitionist newspaper in American history to attract notable national attention. What made it different from other papers and tracts of the day was its abrasive, nonconciliatory tone. In it, Lundy showed no interest in appeasing the slave power of the South, as he believed Henry Clay and the U.S. government had done in the Missouri Compromise. Instead, he published a "Black List" in some editions, detailing various real-life individual cases of slave abuse—murder, torture, and whippings—a dramatic, attention-grabbing tactic that would later be used with even greater effect by Theodore Dwight Weld in his book *Slavery As It Is* in 1839. In 1822, he moved to Greeneville, Tennessee, where he continued publishing the *Genius* and became president of the local chapter of the Tennessee Manumission Society. In 1823, he attended the American Convention for Promoting the Abolition of Slavery in Philadelphia, where he made valuable contacts with like-minded people on the East Coast.

Throughout the 1820s, Lundy traveled the country as an itinerant lecturer and writer, visiting 19 states and holding more than 200 public meetings. He published the *Genius* from wherever he happened to be, which included not only Tennessee in the South but Maryland as well. While in Baltimore, he helped found the Maryland Anti-Slavery Society. He also got beat up by an irate slave holder and sued for libel there. In March 1828, he met the young William Lloyd Garrison, who became his protégé temporarily before striking out on his own. Hiring Garrison to contribute to and run the daily operations of the *Genius* out of Baltimore, Lundy intended to spend more time traveling outside the United States. The association between the two men grew icy, however, because Garrison quickly became more radical than Lundy, and the two disagreed over direction and strategy. Lundy was a gradualist and a colonizationist who had formulated a plan for emancipation as early as 1825, which he remained committed to for the rest of his life, while Garrison became an immediatist.

As a proponent of colonization, Lundy did not necessarily see Africa as the best choice for a colony, as did the American Colonization Society. He considered Haiti, Canada, and the American West as potentially better locations, and he visited all three in person. While he was away on a trip to Haiti, his wife died in childbirth, and he sent his three children to live with relatives. He continued his work unabated, looking for a suitable location for a colony. The West particularly intrigued him. Much like the way the U.S. government had set aside Oklahoma as a supposedly permanent Indian territory, he believed a similar piece of land could be reserved for free blacks. He visited the Mexican frontier region of Texas, which was at that time just beginning to be populated with white Americans, and made great strides toward securing land there for a colony. The outbreak of the Texas Revolution in 1835, however, nixed that idea.

With the victory over Mexico in 1836, the people of Texas applied to the U.S. Congress for admission to the Union as a slave state. This became the next big case in American history in which slavery proved to be a heated political issue, like the Missouri Controversy had been in 1820. Lundy thus started another newspaper, this time in Philadelphia, called the *National Enquirer and Constitutional Advocate of Universal Liberty*, which dealt heavily with the Texas question. He also published a pamphlet called *The War in Texas*, which was devoted to persuading the U.S. government not to annex Texas. It worked, at least for the rest of Lundy's life, although in the end, of course, the United States annexed the Lone Star State. Lundy published the *National Enquirer* for two years before selling it to the renowned Quaker abolitionist poet John Greenleaf Whittier, then moving to north-central Illinois, and restarting the *Genius*. He died there on August 22, 1839.

William Lloyd Garrison (1805–1879)

Born on December 12, 1805, in Newburyport, Massachusetts, William Lloyd Garrison grew up poor and fatherless. Reared by his mother, a devout Baptist, the young Lloyd (as he was known) apprenticed in a local newspaper office for seven years. Working as a typesetter in the early years, he began writing columns for the paper at 16 years old. Writing from a pious Baptist point of view, he shot his first barb at the institution of slavery before his seventeenth birthday. In January 1827, hoping to brighten his career opportunities, he left the small town of Newburyport for the bustling metropolis of Boston. He soon landed the editorship of a failing paper, the *National Philanthropist*, and began to make a name for himself amid considerable competition in the big city.

In March 1828, Garrison met one of the pioneers of the abolition movement, Benjamin Lundy, the Quaker writer of the *Genius of Universal Emancipation*, and the encounter changed his life. From that point on, Garrison was determined to make abolition the one great reform issue of his editorials and the main goal of his life's work. Although he subsequently became the most notable of all abolitionists, he also advocated for a wide variety of other reforms in his columns throughout his career, including temperance, women's rights, pacifism, and anti-Jacksonianism, just to name a few.

On July 4, 1829, Garrison made his debut as a public speaker in Boston, addressing the Congregational Society, a group consisting of some of the most influential of the New England clergy. By then widely known as an antislavery crusader in that region of the country, he moved south to Baltimore, a major slave-holding and slave-trading city, where he took over the editorship of Lundy's *Genius of Universal Emancipation*. He quickly fell afoul of the locals there with the straightforward style of his abolitionist rhetoric, getting sued for libel and being found guilty. He served nearly two months in jail before Arthur Tappan, a wealthy New Yorker and the leader of New York City's abolition group, bailed him out. Thus began his association with Tappan, a very important development in his life and career.

About this same time (1829–1830), Garrison became convinced that immediate emancipation of the slaves, as opposed to gradual emancipation or voluntary manumission, was the best course for abolitionists to pursue. That opinion did not prevail, however, in abolitionist circles, so Garrison became a pioneer in preaching it. To get the message out and to further his career, he founded his own weekly paper, the *Liberator*, in Boston. In the first issue, dated January 1, 1831, he wrote forcefully and famously concerning slavery "I will be as harsh as truth and as uncompromising as justice. . . . AND I WILL BE HEARD." It was the opening salvo of a bombardment of antislavery columns that would be heard again and again for the next 34 years. During that time, the *Liberator* became by far the most influential abolitionist newspaper in the United States, and Garrison became the best known of all abolitionists.

Although Garrison's style was aggressive, controversial, and polarizing, it was not militant. He strongly condemned the use of violence to overthrow slavery, as advocated by David Walker's 1829 pamphlet *Appeal to the Colored Citizens of the World* and as put into action by Nat Turner in 1831 in Virginia. He preached moral suasion instead, which sought to convince readers through rational and religious argumentation that slavery was both a sin a crime against humanity and thereby to work upon their consciences. Regardless, after the Nat Turner revolt, southern political leaders and editors largely blamed him and the *Liberator* for stirring up the slaves to revolt. They put out calls for his arrest, threatened his life, and demanded that the city of Boston shut down his paper. Such acrimony merely served to increase his fame in abolitionist circles.

In 1832, Garrison used his newfound clout to form the New England Antislavery Society (renamed the Massachusetts Antislavery Society in 1836), which, at least in theory, united the various local abolition groups in the Northeast under his leadership. Its first order of business was to denounce the American Colonization Society (ACS) and any schemes for colonizing freed slaves outside the United States via a pamphlet Garrison wrote called *Thoughts on African Colonization*. Before this publication, there had been an alliance of sorts, albeit a tenuous one, between the various opponents of slavery such as colonizationists, gradualists, and immediatists. No more. Garrison ensured that the ACS and his radical wing of the abolition movement would be forever at cross purposes.

In 1833, Garrison attended the World Anti-Slavery Convention in London, which put him at ground zero of the international movement just as Great Britain was abolishing slavery in the British Empire. Although he gained more notoriety and made important contacts, he accomplished little. When he returned to the United States, he joined with the Tappan brothers of New York, the Quakers of Philadelphia, and the evangelicals of Lane Seminary in Cincinnati to form the American Anti-Slavery Society (AASS). Garrison wrote the new organization's "Declaration of Sentiments," in which he proclaimed that "Ours is a moral crusade" and spoke of God, his holy commandments, and repentance. On those points, all members of the AASS agreed. Beyond those points, however, there was friction as the group's various strong-willed personalities clashed over strategy and tactics and as Garrison seemed determined to be in control. Yet the AASS managed to present a fairly united front for several years.

Throughout 1834, Garrison continued to alienate moderate gradualists and colonizationists. In 1835, these moderates formed their own rival abolition group in Boston and sought to depose him from his position of preeminence. Meanwhile, at an abolition lecture in Boston, a lynch mob seized him and nearly succeeded in murdering him. He escaped but spent the night in jail for protection. Rather than letting this close call teach him a lesson or persuade him to ratchet down his radical rhetoric, he turned it into a badge of honor; he claimed to be glad that he was found worthy to suffer for the cause he believed in. In 1837, the State of Massachusetts, under pressure from southern political leaders, called him and fellow radical abolitionists before a committee to investigate what danger, if any, their subversive activities posed. This public reproach at the hands of the government brought many sympathetic people into Garrison's fold.

In 1836, Garrison began to diversify his reform agenda beyond abolitionism in the pages of the *Liberator*. Although he had always been interested in other issues, such as temperance, keeping the Sabbath, and pacifism, he devoted more attention to them now. He also declaimed against cockfighting, tobacco use, and marital infidelity, but more importantly, he began following the teachings of Utopian reformer John Humphrey Noyes, who was even more unorthodox in his social and religious views than Garrison. The most important development in Garrison's life and career at that time, however, was his meeting the Grimke sisters and supporting their controversial appointment as lecturers for the AASS because it put another reform issue—women's rights—squarely in the forefront of his agenda. Although it took another four years to materialize, the women's rights question ultimately contributed to a schism in the AASS, with, essentially, Garrisonians and women on one side and Arthur Tappan and the New York moderates on the other.

In 1840, the split between Garrison and the opposition finally came at the National Convention of Abolitionists, when New Yorkers voted to launch into the deep waters of presidential politics. The Liberty Party was thus created, James G. Birney was nominated, and neither had Garrison's blessing. Thereafter in the 1840s, he continued leading the AASS, publishing the *Liberator*, and making speaking tours throughout the northern states as well as abroad. Meanwhile, he met the most dynamic of all abolitionist orators, Frederick Douglass, and promoted his speaking and writing career until the two had a falling out over Douglass's support of the Liberty Party. Each year that passed, Garrison grew increasingly more radical, repudiating some of his earlier beliefs and even calling for the dissolution of the Union between free states and slave states. The extremely divisive Fugitive Slave Act in the Compromise of 1850 greatly increased his cachet with the northern public, as he said in essence, "I told you so." Not until 1854, however, at Framingham, Massachusetts, did he make the ultimate public show of his disdain for the Union. There, at a Fourth of July celebration, he set the U.S. Constitution on fire and stomped its ashes.

Subsequent events of the late 1850s, such as the Dred Scott ruling and the Harpers Ferry incident, made Garrison's long-time motto "No Union with Slaveholders" seem prophetic. As the 1860s and the Civil War approached, Garrison had become the most notable elder statesman of the abolition movement, although his disciple Wendell Phillips had assumed the position of preeminent spokesman for the Garrisonians. Garrison criticized President Abraham Lincoln for his trepidation in confronting slavery head on but rallied to his side in supporting the war to extirpate slavery from the land. As the war's end approached, Garrison pressed beyond abolition and advocated complete racial equality.

Although he would have cherished the opportunity to spend another decade fighting for equal rights for blacks, when the U.S. government finally passed the 13th Amendment in December 1865, he decided his main life's work was accomplished. He thus stopped the press of the *Liberator* and settled into semi-retirement in Roxbury, Massachusetts. He continued to write for other papers, but the fire in his belly had dwindled down to embers. In 1879, he moved to New York City to spend his last days with his daughter. Within a matter of weeks, he died. He was 73 years old.

The Tappan Brothers: Benjamin (1773–1857), Arthur (1786–1865), and Lewis (1788–1873)

These three brothers—Benjamin, Arthur, and Lewis Tappan—can be considered the "first family" of the abolition movement. Although any one of them could stand alone as an exemplar, their stories so intertwine as to make it simpler to discuss them as a group. All were born in Northampton, Massachusetts, into a strict religious family, and all grew up with a strong social conscience. Although Benjamin was the oldest, Arthur was the real catalyst for abolitionism and reform among the three, and Lewis stayed close by his side, albeit more in the background than on center stage until the 1840s. Whereas Benjamin chose a career in law and politics, Arthur and Lewis became self-made millionaire businessmen. It is necessary herein to discuss the younger brothers first.

Arthur was born on May 22, 1786. He apprenticed in a Boston store, where he learned the business of imports, exports, and wholesaling. In 1826, he started his own business in New York City that imported silk and sold it wholesale to stores in the United States. Lewis, born on May 23, 1788, became his younger business partner. They got rich through their silk enterprise, but they were never greedy or stingy. Rather, they sought ways to use their wealth for magnanimous purposes. They thus supported the American Sunday School Union, American Tract Society, American Education Society, and American Colonization Society early in their careers, as well as Benjamin Lundy's *Genius of Universal Emancipation* in Baltimore and Lane Theological Seminary in Cincinnati.

Arthur and Lewis began as gradualists and colonizationists in the 1820s, as did virtually all abolitionists of that generation. After meeting William Lloyd Garrison, however, and bailing him out of jail, they converted to immediatism and helped fund the creation of Garrison's paper, the *Liberator*. 1833 was in some ways the high point of their career as abolitionists. In that year, the brothers helped fund the creation of Oberlin College near Cleveland, Ohio, which pioneered in being a training school for abolitionists, blacks, and women; they helped found the New York Anti-Slavery Society; and then they teamed up with Garrison, a Bostonian, to create the American Anti-Slavery Society (AASS) in Philadelphia. Arthur served as president of the AASS for seven years, and Lewis was responsible for fund-raising; publication of the society's paper, the *Emancipator*; and the mass mailings of "incendiary" literature, which brought them into conflict with Congress, President Andrew Jackson, and the U.S. postal service in the mid-to late 1830s.

In 1834, anti-abolitionists in New York City targeted Lewis's home for vandalism, but it did not deter him. After a nationwide economic panic sank businesses and ruined fortunes in 1837, Lewis founded the Mercantile Agency, the first credit-rating agency in American history (which evolved into the modern company Dun & Bradstreet, which is today the largest global business information database in the world). Two years later, Lewis threw his moral and financial support behind the Africans in the *Amistad* mutiny case.

In 1840, Arthur and Lewis lost a power struggle with Garrison for control of the AASS. Garrison's increasing radicalism, and their disagreements over direction and strategy, caused the brothers to leave that organization to found the American and Foreign Anti-Slavery Society. They hoped to preserve male hegemony and retain the pure, original moral suasion strategy that had formerly characterized the AASS. In the same year, they helped launch the first national abolitionist political party, the Liberty Party, in New York, which ran James G. Birney for president of the United States.

In 1843, Lewis published a pamphlet called an *Address to the Non-Slaveholders of the South, on the Social and Political Ills of Slavery,* which used the moral suasion technique. Although such an argument potentially could have been effective a decade or two earlier, the time for southerners listening to abolitionist rationales against slavery had passed. Still not deterred, the brothers helped found the American Missionary Association in 1846, which in time sprouted several egalitarian colleges in the South. A year later, they started another abolitionist newspaper, the *National Era,* and donated funds to Frederick Douglass to begin his paper, the *North Star.*

After the new Fugitive Slave Act was passed as part of the Compromise of 1850, Arthur and Lewis began funding the Underground Railroad heavily. In the mid-1850s, Arthur retired from his business and mostly from public life. He lived long enough to see the Civil War come to an end and the slaves set free. He died in New Haven, Connecticut, on July 23, 1865. Lewis lived another five years, just long enough to publish his brother's biography, *The Life of Arthur Tappan,* before dying in Brooklyn, New York, on June 21, 1870.

As Arthur and Lewis's notable lives played out over the decades, their older brother Benjamin was meanwhile working from the bench and various elective offices in the state of Ohio for the abolitionist cause. Yet he held different views about how to achieve the goal. He was a charter member of the Democrat Party in Ohio, a supporter of Andrew Jackson, a constitutional unionist, and a believer in states' rights—a strange combination for an abolitionist. As his one term in the U.S. Senate was ending in 1844 to 1845, he strongly disagreed with his party over the annexation of the slave territory of Texas, so he broke away thereafter and helped form the Free Soil Party in Ohio. He lived long enough thereafter to become a charter member of the Republican Party in Ohio before dying in 1857.

Although Benjamin disagreed with his younger brothers about some key points, his influence as a lawyer, judge, and politician was vitally important in keeping them grounded because they were often surrounded by radicals with all sorts of unorthodox religious and social views. It is truly remarkable that Arthur and Lewis managed to navigate between the mainstream antislavery thought of people like their older brother and still walk in the same circle with people like Garrison and Douglass.

The Grimke Sisters: Sarah (1792–1873) and Angelina (1805–1879)

If the Tappan brothers were the first family of the abolition movement, the Grimke sisters could be considered its second family and its founding mothers. These sisters were born in Charleston, South Carolina, to a liberal Episcopalian family of wealth and influence that boasted 11 children and several slaves. Their father sat on the Palmetto State's Supreme Court. He was an independent thinker who allowed his daughters to receive the same education as his sons. Family gatherings often featured discussions of whatever happened to be making news at the time, and the girls participated on an equal footing with the boys. Consequently, the girls grew up with a mind for public service and social reform at a time when females doing such things was taboo in American society. Sarah dreamed of becoming a lawyer (later she decided she wanted to be a doctor), but the country was not ready to accept women into those professions yet, and her father discouraged her from that pursuit.

Born on November 26, 1792, Sarah Moore Grimke was 12 years older than Angelina Emily Grimke, who was born on February 20, 1805. Because her mother had her hands full with rearing children, Sarah became the primary caregiver for little Angelina, who saw her older sister as more of a mother than a sibling. In fact, Angelina referred to Sarah as "Mother" for many years. Despite the age difference, the sisters had much in common. Their personalities were in some ways opposites, but they were also complementary. Sarah was studious, contemplative, and somewhat introverted, and Angelina was effervescent, playful, and outspoken. Not surprisingly, after they began their careers as abolitionists, Sarah became primarily a researcher and writer who dealt in facts about slavery and approached the topic politically and theologically, and Angelina became a lecturer and writer who emoted, opined, and appealed to her audiences' feelings more than their intellect.

As a child growing up with slavery all around her, Sarah always disliked the mistreatment of slaves that she routinely witnessed, as well as the occasional beatings and outlandish abuses of various kinds. In childhood, she once received a slave (personal servant) as a gift. She treated her slave as an equal and a family member. As she grew older, the whole concept of white superiority and black victimization troubled her conscience more and more. Upon making her first trip outside the South in 1820, she met a Quaker preacher who changed her life, transforming her into an ardent abolitionist. She thus packed up and moved to Philadelphia to live among the Friends and to prepare for a career in ministry. Unfortunately, despite their liberality on racial equality and a number of other social issues, they would not allow women to speak at their meetings. Devastated and confused, when she finally did get the chance to speak publicly years later on the abolition lecture circuit, she focused just as much on women's rights as on slavery.

Meanwhile, back in Charleston, as Angelina came of age, she joined the Presbyterian Church in 1826. Her outspoken and self-righteous demeanor was not welcome there, however, and in 1829 she left for Philadelphia to be with her sister and to join the Society of Friends. She attended her first formal abolition meeting in 1835 and was so enthralled that she wrote a letter to William Lloyd Garrison, editor of the *Liberator*, expressing her views on slavery. So impressed was Garrison that he published her letter in his paper, making the young lady an instant celebrity in abolitionist circles. Thus began her writing career and her public life as an abolitionist. She soon published an *Appeal to the Christian Women of the South* (1836) and an *Appeal to the Women of the Nominally Free States* (1837), both of which used moral suasion to tug at the heartstrings of her fellow females. Sarah likewise published *An Epistle to the*

Clergy of the Southern States (1836) as a series of articles in abolitionist papers, which argued against slavery and gender inequality by parsing Bible verses dealing with each.

Although Philadelphia had important, active abolitionist groups in the mid-1830s, the Quakers were modest and conservative in their fight against slavery. After attending a meeting of the American Anti-Slavery Society in 1836 and meeting a more radical, belligerent, and immediatist style of abolitionism, the sisters joined up with the Tappan brothers and the New York Anti-Slavery Society and were employed by them in 1837 as the first female lecturers in American history. They spoke at first only to female audiences, but as converts from a southern slave-holding family, they piqued such interest that men began attending their lectures, too, and soon they were speaking before mixed audiences. On July 17, 1837, Angelina even debated a man publicly on slavery, a first in American history. In February 1838, in Massachusetts, she became the first woman to speak before a state legislature on slavery. Such cutting-edge social change did not go unchallenged. In Philadelphia, on November 28, 1838, an angry mob torched the building in protest of these abolitionist sisters' public speaking.

In 1838, each sister published another book. Sarah's was *Letters on the Equality of the Sexes and the Condition of Women*, and Angelina's was *Letters to Catherine Beecher*. The latter argued various points pertaining to abolitionism, as well as for the right of women to speak publicly to mixed audiences. It was addressed to the influential educator Catherine Beecher of Boston, who, despite being from a prominent family of abolitionists, criticized the Grimkes for their outspokenness. By this time, the women's rights issue had become so entangled with the abolition movement that it was causing a great deal of consternation to the Tappan brothers and fellow moderates. The problem was partly solved when the prominent abolitionist Theodore Dwight Weld, with whom the sisters had been collaborating on a book, asked Angelina to marry him. Despite the fact that Weld was Presbyterian and she would be expelled from the Society of Friends, she accepted. The couple was wed on May 14, 1838. They bought a farm in New Jersey and had children, and both sisters soon left the public sphere and settled into domestic life.

Weld's book, *Slavery As It Is: Testimony of a Thousand Witnesses*, appeared in 1839 and immediately became the most powerful and damning polemic against slavery produced up until that time. Each sister contributed her personal recollections of slavery from childhood, as well as their intimate knowledge of the mind of slave holders. Their testimonies bolstered the book's case considerably. The book served as a capstone for their half-decade of public life, and they could retire thereafter knowing they had done more than most abolitionists would achieve in a lifetime. They spent the remainder of their lives mostly out of the spotlight, teaching in various schools opened or managed by Weld, and making their final home in Massachusetts.

James G. Birney (1792–1857)

Born on February 4, 1792, in Danville, Kentucky, to a slave-holding family, James Gillespie Birney became a slave holder himself at the tender age of 6 years, receiving human property as an inheritance. Similar to his father and other more famous slave holders before him, such as Thomas Jefferson, he became an apologetic owner of slaves. He opposed the institution in theory and wished it had never arisen in the United States, but he refused to free his slaves for many years because he believed they were better off under a kind master than being forced to fend for themselves as free blacks in a hostile land. (He still owned 21 slaves who were valued at $20,000 in 1839, when he finally set them free.) Yet influenced by the antislavery Methodist preachers David Barrow and David Rice in the Bluegrass State, his theoretical abolitionist beliefs grew stronger as the years went by, even as he curiously acquired more slaves through marriage.

After studying at Princeton in New Jersey and Transylvania College in Kentucky, among other places, Birney became a lawyer in his hometown. He was almost immediately elected to the state legislature, where he sided with the antislavery minority on the issue of free states returning slaves to Kentucky under the Fugitive Slave Law of 1793. Ironically, this antislavery slave holder soon left the upper South and moved into the heart of Dixie to become a plantation owner in Alabama. Again, almost immediately, he won a seat in the state legislature, where he sided with an even smaller antislavery minority. He also helped found the University of Alabama. His opposition to the burgeoning political career of the great war hero Andrew Jackson, however, killed his own political career in Alabama. And his plantation did not fare well, so he went back to practicing law and moved back to Kentucky.

At about the same time, in the early 1820s, the American Colonization Society (ACS) was beginning its thrust to relocate freed slaves in Liberia, and Birney saw that as a viable option. He advocated it, along with voluntary, gradual manumission, for several years unofficially before taking a job as an agent for the ACS in 1832, when he began touring the country lecturing to that effect. He did not stay in that position long, however, because his views were constantly evolving, and he soon came to believe that only a forced and enforced, legally required emancipation would ever end slavery in America. He quit the ACS in 1834, therefore, and soon joined the ranks of the American Anti-Slavery Society (AASS). He then intended to start an antislavery newspaper in Danville, but proslavery townspeople threatened his life, so he decided to move north instead.

Settling in New Richmond, Ohio, Birney started a paper called the *Philanthropist* in 1836. Before long, however, he relocated his operations to Cincinnati, where his press was destroyed, his property was vandalized, and he was publicly jeered on more than one occasion. Meanwhile, in 1837, he left his paper in the hands of an assistant and moved to New York City to become the director of the AASS. Although he had many supporters in that organization, within three years, he had clashed with William Lloyd Garrison and other radicals in the AASS over direction and strategy. Birney was a moderate and wanted to find a way to end slavery and preserve the Union under the U.S. Constitution, which largely contributed to his faction—which was headed by the Tappan brothers—breaking away from the AASS in 1840, forming the American and Foreign Anti-Slavery Society, and founding the Liberty Party.

At the same time the party was being organized, Birney was traveling abroad to speak at the World Anti-Slavery Convention in London, and he was publishing a book called *The American Churches: The Bulwarks of American Slavery*. Returning to the United States,

Birney did not seek the nomination for president of the United States on the Liberty Party ticket, but he was nominated nonetheless. He initially declined, but when his supporters persisted, he acquiesced. In the November 1840 election, not surprisingly, his name was not even listed on southern state ballots, and he garnered barely 7,000 votes. The party faithful were not deterred by this low number but rather resolved to make a better showing in 1844. They nominated Birney again, and this time he received about 62,000 votes. Although not nearly enough to win the election, it was just enough to swing the election away from the Whig candidate, Henry Clay, and give it to the dark horse Democrat, James K. Polk.

Meanwhile, Birney moved to Michigan. Now in his fifties, his health began to deteriorate, resulting from a fall that left him partially paralyzed. He spent his last days writing antislavery articles and pamphlets, but he otherwise withdrew from public life. He died in Perth Amboy, New Jersey, at 65 years of age.

Frederick Douglass (1818–1895)

Frederick Douglass was born Frederick Augustus Washington Bailey in Talbot County, Maryland, just across the Chesapeake Bay from Baltimore. His date of birth is not known for certain, but is thought to be February 1818. His father's identity is likewise not known for a fact but is suspected to have been his white owner, Aaron Anthony, who was a slave holder, a small farmer, and an overseer for local planters. His mother was a slave named Harriet Bailey, but Frederick barely knew her, because she was hired out to a different plantation and died when he was a child. His maternal grandmother was his actual caregiver until he was about 7 years old, and they lived on the tobacco plantation of Edward Lloyd. There Douglass first encountered the rigorous work routine and harsh discipline that typified plantation life for slaves, although he mostly observed it rather than being personally subjected to it.

In 1825, Anthony sent Douglass to a new home in Baltimore, where he was trained to be a house servant for Hugh Auld and family. There he was given charge of watching over Auld's youngest son. Auld's wife, Sophia, felt compassion and affection for little "Freddie" and began teaching him to read and write, which did not meet with the master's approval. Denied any more lessons, the youngster sneaked around, picked up school books, and finished teaching himself how to read and write.

After several years, Hugh Auld's brother, Thomas, took Douglass to live in the country with him. The two did not get along because Thomas was determined to instill discipline in the teenager. He thus sent him to a locally-famous "slave-breaker" named Covey, who was a poor farmer, for a life lesson. There he was made to do grueling outdoor work and to be subject to the lash if he did not perform up to Covey's standards. Living and working for Covey for several months indeed took a toll on Douglass, but rather than breaking him, it made him determined to fight back against what he considered cruel and inhumane treatment. When, at about age 16, he beat the grown white man in a hand-to-hand scuffle, he discovered his own physical strength, and no man dared to whip him again.

Thereafter, Douglass went through a series of different employers, being hired out by one or the other of the Auld brothers for the next four years. On his first job at a Baltimore shipyard, Douglass got into a fight with fellow workers, who nearly killed him. He subsequently went to work at another shipyard where he fared much better. With each passing job in every new location, he gained knowledge of the world that he would later use to plan his escape. His first attempted escape failed, however, as he and his companions were caught and thrown in jail until they were claimed by their masters. Finally, on September 3, 1838, he succeeded at escaping aboard a ship moving up the Delaware River. He made it to Philadelphia and on to New York, where he changed his name to Douglass and began living the life of a fugitive slave.

In August 1841, Douglass met William Lloyd Garrison for the first time at an antislavery convention at Nantucket, Massachusetts. Immediately impressed, Garrison hired Douglass as a lecturer for the Massachusetts Anti-Slavery Society. His striking appearance was simultaneously powerful and graceful. His oratorical skills were a diamond in the rough, soon to be polished by more than 1,000 public addresses over the course of his career. His personal testimony of life in slavery mesmerized white northern audiences. Many listeners had never heard a black man take the stage and speak, and the force of Douglass's words struck them like lightning. Before hearing him, in some cases, whites questioned whether blacks had the ability to become leaders in society; after hearing him, they could not doubt it.

In 1843, Douglass traveled to Great Britain, where he toured Ireland and England, meeting fellow abolitionists, giving speeches, and arousing a great deal of sympathy for his condition. His British friends thus raised money to buy his freedom. He returned to the United States and settled down in Rochester, New York, which lay in the heart of the "burnt-over district" of religious fervor and social reform movements. In 1845, he published his first autobiography, and still the one for which he is best known, *The Narrative of the Life of Frederick Douglass, An American Slave*. It was a smash hit with both the American and British public. Within five years, it had sold 30,000 copies worldwide. He later published two other memoirs, *My Bondage and My Freedom* (1855) and the *Life and Times of Frederick Douglass* (1881).

Meanwhile, in 1847, he and two partners began publishing their own abolitionist weekly paper, the *North Star*, against the wishes of William Lloyd Garrison and the American Anti-Slavery Society. Garrison's two main objections to the paper were that Douglass's time would be better spent making public appearances on the lecture circuit and that he had no experience in the newspaper business and thus should leave it to the experts (with himself being the chief expert in the abolitionist newspaper publishing business). Truthfully, Garrison did not want more competition. Douglass broke from his mentor over this point, however, as well as over the radical, anti–U.S. Constitution rhetoric Garrison used in his *Liberator* and in his public addresses and over the question of whether abolitionists should be involved in national politics. Douglass threw his support behind the Liberty Party of James G. Birney, which put him in league with Garrison's big rivals, the Tappan brothers and the American and Foreign Anti-Slavery Society. Douglass needed the support of the Tappans and other wealthy allies to keep his struggling paper afloat. In 1851, he merged his paper with their *Liberty Party Paper* and formed *Frederick Douglass' Paper*, which continued operating until 1860, when it switched to a monthly publication called *Douglass' Monthly*, until it folded three years later.

Soon after Douglass began his newspaper business, he attended the now-famous women's rights conference at Seneca Falls, New York, where he gave his support to that cause. He was the only black person present. He signed the women's Declaration of Sentiments and wrote and spoke favorably thereafter about women's rights being part of the broader reform movement of guaranteeing equal rights for all people, of which abolitionism was the most pressing example at the time.

In 1859, the militant abolitionist John Brown, who had already murdered five men in Kansas three years earlier, came to Douglass to enlist his aid for a plan to start a slave revolt. Douglass, a man of peaceful protest, listened to the plan but totally rejected it. He implored Brown not to do it. Brown carried out the plan anyway, staging his infamous raid on Harpers Ferry, Virginia. Douglass, fearing he would be implicated in the plot, fled to Canada for a while. Soon after, Abraham Lincoln was elected president of the United States, the Civil War began, and the questions of slavery and racial equality were thrust to the fore. Douglass became an advisor to Lincoln and a recruiter of black soldiers for the Union Army, helping raise the historic Massachusetts 54th regiment.

After the war, Douglass enjoyed a long and mostly rewarding career, although the objective he spent the rest of his life fighting for—racial equality—was not realized in his time. Still, he played an instrumental role in the Freedman's Bureau, he served as a U.S. marshal for the District of Columbia, and he earned an appointment as the U.S. Minister to Haiti. He died in Washington, D.C., on February 20, 1895.

Wendell Phillips (1811–1884)

Born into a wealthy political family in Boston on November 29, 1811, Wendell Phillips was the youngest of 11 children. He attended Harvard University, graduating with a law degree in 1833. Although he tried to pursue a legal career, he quickly became infatuated with the nobility of purpose espoused by William Lloyd Garrison and fellow abolitionists. The attempted lynching of Garrison in Boston in 1835 by an anti-abolitionist mob converted him to the cause. In 1836, he fell in love with a Garrisonian named Ann Terry Greene and joined the American Anti-Slavery Society and the Massachusetts Anti-Slavery Society. He supported the Free Produce movement, boycotting products grown by slave labor. His first claim to fame came on December 8, 1837, at a meeting at Faneuil Hall in Boston in which the murder of Elijah Lovejoy was the topic of discussion. There he delivered an unprepared speech, stunning in its eloquence and articulation, denouncing the proslavery murderers and extolling Lovejoy as a martyr. He thus began to acquire the nickname "the golden trumpet" and to be something like Garrison's right-hand man.

In the tumultuous split in the American Anti-Slavery Society in 1840, Phillips remained on Garrison's team. The two men worked together and agreed upon about as much as any two abolitionists possibly could. Similar to Garrison, Phillips believed the U.S. Constitution was a proslavery document and that men of conscience in the North should not vote or hold office in the U.S. government. In 1842 and 1843, he wrote pamphlets to that effect entitled *The Constitution—A Proslavery Document* and *Can Abolitionists Vote or Hold Office Under the United States Constitution?* Moreover, he favored northern state secession from the Union as the immediate remedy for that problem. He did not approve, however, when the southern states were the ones to secede in 1860 and 1861; instead, he deemed it treason. By then, unlike the pacifistic Garrison, he espoused the use of force to achieve abolition.

Phillips's reputation as an orator grew considerably in the 1850s as he embarked on the abolitionist lecture circuit and got involved in the Boston Vigilance Committee's attempts to rescue fugitive slaves such as Anthony Burns. In his public speaking engagements, he always carried a radical message, but he typically delivered his points in a calm, contemplative manner spiced with anecdotes and humor. He spoke plainly and was not prone to high rhetorical flourishes so common in that generation, although some of his famous quotes come across that way today. Consequently, his logic was easier to follow than that of many abolitionists, including his mentor Garrison. He generally did not get sidetracked by other social reform issues, and he had a more likeable personality and style than Garrison. Among white American abolitionists, he was unrivaled as a speaker. The only thing missing from his arsenal of oratory was the first-hand slave experience that Frederick Douglass and other black speakers brought to the stage.

Phillips made a seamless transition from abolitionism to civil rights and racial equality advocacy during the Civil War. He criticized the Lincoln administration for moving too slowly in freeing the slaves and not doing enough to ensure the former slaves' welfare thereafter. He thus strongly supported all three Reconstruction amendments. Even after the ratification of the 13th Amendment, he, unlike Garrison, did not consider his work done. He continued after Garrison's retirement to publish the *Liberator* for five more years. Not until after the 15th Amendment was ratified was he satisfied that he had done his duty to God and humankind on the issue of racial justice and equality. He spent the remainder of his life working for other causes, such as women's rights, worker's rights, and justice and fair treatment for American Indians. One of his oft-quoted statements proved to be prophetic: "What is fanaticism today is the fashionable creed tomorrow." He died on February 2, 1884, in Boston.

John Brown (1800–1859)

Born on May 9, 1800, in Torrington, Connecticut, into a Christian family of old Puritan stock, John Brown's father moved the family of seven to Ohio in 1805. There he opened a tannery and became acquainted with some of the evangelical people and institutions that would later be driving forces for the abolition movement. Brown thus learned tanning, radical religious views, and hatred for slavery as a child, and all would be important parts of his life as an adult. He briefly lived in the home of future U.S. president and Civil War hero Ulysses S. Grant. In 1816, as a teenager, he moved to Massachusetts and then to Connecticut to study for the ministry. It did not work out, so he headed back west for Ohio.

In 1820, Brown married his first wife and fathered the first of 20 children he would have altogether with two wives. In 1825, he moved to Pennsylvania and started a farm and a tannery, and he soon tried his hand at various other ways to make a living, but illness and the death of his first wife and one of his children conspired against him. In 1836, he moved to Ohio and continued his experiments to make money, but he went bankrupt within six years. Moving from state to state and occupation to occupation proved a lifelong pattern for him.

Although Brown had always abhorred slavery, his conversion to becoming an active abolitionist came after the infamous murder of

Elijah P. Lovejoy in Alton, Illinois, in 1837. He vowed thereafter to spend the rest of his life fighting the diabolical institution that caused such heinous crimes and kept millions in bondage. He had radical tendencies all along, but each passing year brought his abolitionist ideology into sharper focus. Within a decade, he had decided nothing less than a slave revolt complete with the shedding of blood would end slavery in the United States.

Influenced by militant blacks such as David Walker and Henry Highland Garnet, Brown was one of the few white men who had the courage of his convictions to carry out the grand plan he envisioned. Meeting Frederick Douglass for the first time in 1847, Brown told him of his plan. Although he was not able to carry out that original plan, he never stopped thinking of ways to modify it to bring it to fruition someday. Twelve years in the making, it ultimately evolved into the blueprint for his raid on Harpers Ferry.

Meanwhile, unable to stay in one place very long, Brown moved to Massachusetts in 1846, where he ventured into a business partnership that proved financially disastrous and kept him in legal turmoil for several years. In 1848, he moved to the Adirondack Mountains of upstate New York to help the wealthy abolitionist and leader of the Liberty Party Gerrit Smith establish his free black and fugitive black commune of Timbuktoo. It failed, however, and Brown again found himself a man in search of a home and a job. Even so, he had made an important connection with Smith and his circle of New York abolitionists, and he would forever be linked with them.

As the politics of slavery in the 1850s began to polarize Americans more than ever before, Brown and some of his grown sons got involved in the campaign to help make Kansas a free state. The sons moved to Kansas amid the growing tension there, and the father became an agent of the Kansas Aid Society of Massachusetts. He took people and supplies to Kansas in 1855 and soon clashed with proslavery border ruffians. On May 24, 1856, he led a group of abolitionists to kill five proslavery men at Pottawatomie Creek. The violence in Kansas only increased thereafter, and he and his band had another bloody clash with proslavery forces at Osawatomie in August. There he began to acquire nicknames that would follow him from then on: "Osawatomie Brown" and "Captain John Brown." Although the Kansas campaign was not what he had envisioned years earlier as the method he would use to end slavery in the United States, it put blood on his hands for the first time and set him on the path toward his doom.

In 1856 and 1857, Brown moved repeatedly back and forth from Kansas and the Great Plains region to the Midwest, New York, and New England. He made connections with leading abolitionists, recruited followers for his "army," and raised money to fight his war, which resulted in his making an alliance with a group that came to be known as the Secret Six. This group of wealthy, influential men accepted and encouraged his plan to start a slave revolt in the South. Of the six, the Unitarian minister Thomas Wentworth Higginson especially gave him moral support to stick with the plan, and the businessman George Luther Stearns provided him with money and weapons.

In 1858, Brown met with Frederick Douglass at his Rochester, New York, home to enlist his support for the Harpers Ferry raid, but Douglass refused. He then went to Canada where he held an abolitionist meeting in Chatham, Ontario. There he and his comrades drew up a new U.S. Constitution that prohibited slavery and elected themselves to various high offices in the new provisional government. His next step was to continue the Kansas campaign by going to Missouri, killing a slave holder, and leading a small group of slaves to their freedom in Canada.

Early in 1859, in the midst of his last whirlwind fund-raising tour of the Northeast, he traveled to Harpers Ferry, Virginia, to scope out the town and finalize the plan.

Situated at the edge of the Appalachian Mountains, where the Shenandoah River rushes violently into the Potomac River, about 75 miles east of Washington, D.C., Harpers Ferry was the place that Thomas Jefferson once said was one of the most picturesque he had ever seen. From this small town, Lewis and Clark had met up to begin their journey westward in 1804 exploring the Louisiana Territory. As of 1859, it was home to a U.S. Army weapons foundry and arsenal, which is one reason Brown chose it as ground zero for his slave revolt—for the availability of weapons with which to arm the slaves. The other reason was that it lay barely 15 miles south of the Mason-Dixon Line, and he could get a foothold into the South there without getting caught.

Finally, in October 1859, Brown was ready to implement his long-awaited slave revolt. He took his army of 13 whites and five blacks to Harpers Ferry on October 16, along with a wagon load of 200 "Beecher's Bibles" (Sharps .52 caliber rifles). The Brown gang cut the telegraph lines leading out of town, killed a railroad worker aboard a train headed for Washington, D.C., and seized the armory and two adjacent buildings in the small town. They took hostages, one of whom was Lewis Washington, a kinsman of the legendary Founding Father and U.S. President George Washington. They then issued a call around the town for local blacks to join them, but none did. Local whites soon surrounded them instead and began shooting. Taking refuge inside the small fire engine house, they holed up all night. By the next morning, the U.S. marines, headed by the not-yet-famous Colonel Robert E. Lee, arrived and took command of the situation. Lee and his lieutenant J. E. B. Stuart gave Brown an opportunity to surrender, but Brown refused. A part standoff, part shootout then ensued, in which one soldier perished and about a dozen of Brown's men were killed, including two of his sons. In the end, Brown was wounded, and as he lay helpless on the ground, with the point of a marine's sword at his throat, Lee ordered him arrested rather than killed.

The legal system moved much more swiftly in those days than it does today. Brown stood trial in Virginia state court at the nearby city of Charles Town just two weeks after he was captured. The trial was short; the verdict was easy to reach. The southern proslavery jury found him guilty of murder, treason, and inciting a slave insurrection. The sentence for such crimes was death. Brown took advantage of the opportunity to make a final statement before he left the courtroom. He claimed he never intended to kill anyone but that casualties were the result of necessity rather than choice. His only aim was to free the slaves. He used his understanding of the Bible as the justification for his actions. He added, "Now, if it is deemed necessary that I should forfeit my life for the furtherance of the ends of justice, and mingle my blood further with the blood of millions in this slave country whose rights are disregarded by wicked, cruel, and unjust enactments,—I submit; so let it be done!" He ended by commending the court for its fairness and civil treatment of him.

As he awaited his day of execution, he wrote eloquent letters that became testaments to his sincere beliefs, which later served to rally sympathizers to the abolition movement. One month after his trial, on December 2, 1859, John Brown went to the gallows. Interestingly, at his execution were men who would later become legends, Thomas "Stonewall" Jackson and John Wilkes Booth. With them, so many strands of history converged into one time and place with John Brown at Harpers Ferry—from the nexus to George Washington and Thomas Jefferson, to the Confederate and Union military leadership connection, to the link to the assassin of the man who would ultimately free the slaves.

One major, tragic consequence of Brown's last action was that it hastened the splitting of the United States by enraging southerners and giving them the impression that all abolitionists were like John Brown and that most northerners approved of what he did. As a result, towns all over the South began arming themselves and building their local militias to combat any future abolitionist zealots who would dare to continue Brown's work, thus ensuring that the South would be well-armed for the long Civil War to come. When the war came, Brown's memory would be invoked by Union soldiers in the song whose words rang out, "John Brown's body lies a-moulderin' in the grave, but his soul is marching on." Although the origin of the song is dubious and probably was not written with this particular "John Brown" in mind, the words certainly applied to him after the fact. Abolitionist author Julia Ward Howe, wife of Samuel Gridley Howe, who was one of the Secret Six, later turned that tune into one of the greatest patriotic songs in American history, "The Battle Hymn of the Republic."

Because the saga of John Brown ended so close to the outbreak of the Civil War, Brown was, for all intents and purposes, the last of the abolitionists to make an appearance on the stage of history. It is somehow fitting that this man who came last in a long line of abolitionists embodied all of the most radical and fanatical elements of the movement in one. It is difficult to imagine that the bloody war that raged between the North and South for four years, that killed 625,000 Americans and left another 300,000 wounded, and that ultimately brought the demise of slavery would have happened without a John Brown figure on the pages of history.

Primary Documents

John Woolman, A Quaker Abolitionist, Argues with Proslavery Apologists about the Bible (1757)

John Woolman (1720–1772) was a Quaker from New Jersey who traveled throughout the American colonies preaching and teaching and frequently declaiming against slavery. The journal he kept is a classic of American literature, offering an important glimpse into colonial life. The following passage, circa 1757, shows how ignorance of the Bible fostered certain proslavery ideas even among the generally well-educated Society of Friends (Quakers) and how antislavery people like Woolman had to struggle patiently against such ignorance. Striking is the fact that the same biblical canard cited here in colonial times—the "Curse of Ham"—for justifying slavery would continue to be recited again and again by every succeeding generation on the proslavery side, meaning abolitionists could never put it to rest. Consequently, it continued to circulate even after 1865, being adopted by white supremacists to justify postslavery racial discrimination.

"Having traveled through Maryland, we came amongst Friends at Cedar Creek in Virginia. . . . a Friend in company began to talk in support of the slave-trade, and said the negroes were understood to be the offspring of Cain, their blackness being the mark which God set upon him after he murdered Abel, his brother; that it was the design of Providence they should be slaves, as a condition proper to the race of so wicked a man as Cain was. Then another spake in support of what had been said.

"To all which I replied in substance as follows: that Noah and his family were all who survived the flood, according to Scripture; and as Noah was of Seth's race, the family of Cain was wholly destroyed. One of them said that after the flood Ham went to the land of Nod and took a wife; that Nod was a land far distant, inhabited by Cain's race, and that the flood did not reach it; and as Ham was sentenced to be a servant of servants to his brethren, these two families, being thus joined, were undoubtedly fit only for slaves. I replied, the flood was a judgment upon the world for their abominations, and it was granted that Cain's stock was the most wicked, and therefore unreasonable to suppose that they were spared. As to Ham's going to the land of Nod for a wife, no time being fixed, Nod might be inhabited by some of Noah's family before Ham married a second time; moreover the text saith, 'That all flesh died that moved upon the earth' (Gen. vii.21). I further reminded them how the prophets repeatedly declare 'that the son shall not suffer for the iniquity of the father, but every one be answerable for his own sins.'"

"I was troubled to perceive the darkness of their imaginations, and in some pressure of spirit said, 'The love of ease and gain are the motives in general of keeping slaves, and men are wont to take hold of weak arguments to support a cause which is unreasonable.'"

Source: Excerpt from John Woolman, *The Journal and Other Writings of John Woolman.* London: J. M. Dent & Sons, 1910.

David Walker, A Free Black, Appeals to the Slaves to Get Militant (1829)

David Walker was a free black man born in the South who lived in Boston in the late 1820s. Having traveled the country and seen the evils of slavery up close, he took a militant position against the institution. In his Appeal to the Coloured Citizens of the World, *he urged his fellow blacks to fight and kill whites if necessary to liberate themselves rather than submit to the dehumanizing effects of slavery. In 1830, not surprisingly, he became the South's greatest villain. Some southern states even put a large bounty on his head— dead or alive. He refused to flee to safety, however, but stood his ground in Boston. Evidence suggests that Walker was dying of tuberculosis when he wrote the* Appeal, *so he did not fear what might happen to him for publishing such a shocking treatise. Within the year, he was dead, but his* Appeal *came to life in the form of the Nat Turner rebellion within another year.*

"My dearly beloved Brethren and Fellow Citizens.

"HAVING travelled [*sic*] over a considerable portion of these United States, and having, in the course of my travels, taken the most accurate observations of things as they exist—the result of my observations has warranted the full and unshaken conviction, that we, (coloured people of these United States,) are the most degraded, wretched, and abject set of beings that ever lived since the world began. . . .

. . .

" . . . Can our condition be any worse?—Can it be more mean and abject? . . . . Can they get us any lower? Where can they get us? They are afraid to treat us worse, for they know well, the day they do it they are gone. . . .

. . .

" . . . if you can only get courage into the blacks, I do declare it, that one good black man can put to death six white men; and I give it as a fact, let twelve black men get well armed for battle, and they will kill and put to flight fifty whites.—The reason is, the blacks, once you get them started, they glory in death. The whites have had us under them for more than three centuries, murdering, and treating us like brutes . . . if you commence, make sure work—do not trifle, for they will not trifle with you—they want us for their slaves, and think nothing of murdering us in order to subject us to that wretched condition—therefore, if there is an *attempt* made by us, kill or be killed. Now, I ask you, had you not rather be killed than to be a slave to a tyrant, who takes the life of your mother, wife, and dear little children? Look upon your mother, wife and children, and answer God Almighty; and believe this, that it is no more harm for you to kill a man, who is trying to kill you, than it is for you to take a drink of water when thirsty; in fact, the man who will stand still and let another murder him, is worse than an infidel, and, if he has common sense, ought not to be pitied.

. . .

"Men of colour, who are also of sense, for you particularly is my APPEAL designed. Our more ignorant brethren are not able to penetrate its value. I call upon you therefore to cast your eyes upon the wretchedness of your brethren, and to do your utmost to enlighten them—*go to work and enlighten your brethren!* ..."

Source: Excerpts from David Walker, *Walker's Appeal, in Four Articles; Together with a Preamble, to the Coloured Citizens of the World, but in Particular, and Very Expressly, to Those of the United States of America.* Boston, 1829. Available at http://docsouth.unc.edu/nc/walker/menu.html

William Lloyd Garrison, A Radical Abolitionist, Rejects Manumission and Colonization (1830)

Over a career spanning more than three decades, William Lloyd Garrison became synonymous with the abolition movement. His earliest antislavery editorials were written not for his own paper but for his mentor's—Benjamin Lundy's Genius of Universal Emancipation. *Lundy was an advocate of manumission and colonization. In the following excerpts from February 19, 1830, less than a year before he exploded on the scene with his own paper, the* Liberator, *the fiery young Garrison shows his first radical departure from antislavery conventional wisdom by rejecting manumission and colonization on the grounds that most slaveholders will never be persuaded to give up their human property. They would, instead, justify holding them in bondage through an argument of paternalism.*

"It is morally impossible, I am convinced, for a slaveholder to reason correctly on the subject of slavery. His mind is warped by a thousand prejudices, and a thick cloud rests upon his mental vision. He was really taught to believe, that a certain class of beings were born for servitude, whom it is lawful to enthral [*sic*], and over whom he is authorized—not merely by the law of his native state, but by Jehovah himself—to hold unlimited dominion. His manhood, perhaps, may detect the absurdity of the doctrine, but interest weakens the force of conviction, and he is never at a loss to find palliatives for his conduct. He discourses eloquently, it may be, upon the evils of the system—deprecates its continuance as a curse upon the country— shudders when he contemplates individual instances of barbarity— and rejoices in gradual emancipation. [Yet] Interrogate him relative to his own practices, and you touch the apple of his eye. ... he takes shelter in the ignorance and helplessness of his slaves; and dextrously [*sic*] relinquishing the authority of an oppressor, assumes the amiableness of a philanthropist! 'The poor creatures are penny-less [*sic*]—benighted—without a home! Freedom would be a curse, rather than a blessing to them—they are happy now—why should I throw them upon an unpitying world?' Will a christian reason in this manner? Yes—if a christian can be a slaveholder—but the two characters differ so widely, that I know not how they can unite in one man. Yet this wicked cant obtains as readily at the north as the south, and with many it is as impregnable as the rock of Gibraltar."

Source: Excerpt from William Lloyd Garrison, *Genius of Universal Emancipation.* Baltimore, MD, February 19, 1830.

The Objective and Methodology of the American Anti-Slavery Society (1833)

On December 4, 1833, delegates from various smaller abolitionist organizations met in Philadelphia and formed the American Anti-Slavery Society (AASS). The AASS immediately became a great catalyzing force in the abolition movement. Under the guidance of William Lloyd Garrison, it adopted a Declaration of Sentiments containing a constitution that stated its purpose and methods. This excerpt shows plainly what that purpose would be and what its main method of achieving it would be.

"Art. I—This Society shall be called the American Anti-Slavery Society.

"Art. II—The object of this Society is the entire abolition of Slavery in the United States. While it admits that each State, in which Slavery exists, has, by the Constitution of the United States, the exclusive right to *legislate* in regard to its abolition in said State, it shall aim to convince all our fellow-citizens, by arguments addressed to their understandings and consciences, that Slaveholding is a heinous crime in the sight of God

. . . "

Source: "The American Anti-Slavery Society: Constitution," cited in Henry Steele Commager, ed. *Documents of American History.* New York: Appleton-Century-Crofts, 7th ed., 1963.

John C. Calhoun, A Powerful Southern Senator, Criticizes the Abolitionists (1837)

John C. Calhoun was a U. S. Senator from South Carolina, a planta-
tion owner, and a slave holder. Rather than making excuses for the
South's peculiar institution, in the 1830s and -1840s, he became one
of the most powerful spokesmen for its being a "positive good" for
America. As the U.S. government under President Andrew Jackson
sought ways to limit or mitigate the abolition movement, Calhoun
sponsored a bill in 1837 that would have given states the authority
to stop antislavery literature from being transmitted through the
U.S. Mail. The reasons he gave for doing so follow herein.

"The blindness of fanaticism is proverbial. With more zeal than
understanding, it constantly misconceives the nature of the object
at which it aims, and toward which it rushes with headlong violence,
regardless of the means by which it is effected.—Never was its character more fully exemplified than in the present instance. Setting out
with the abstract principle that slavery is evil, the fanatical zealots
come at once to the conclusion that it is their duty to abolish it,
regardless of the disasters which must follow. Never was conclusion
more false or dangerous.

"Wicked and cruel as is the end aimed at, it is fully equalled [*sic*] by
the criminality of the means by which it is proposed to be accomplished. These consist in organized societies and a powerful press,
directed mainly with a view to excite the bitterest animosity and
hatred of the people of the non-slaveholding States against the citizens and institutions of the slaveholding States. It is easy to see what
disastrous results such means must tend.—The incessant action of
hundreds of societies, and a vast printing establishment, throwing
out, daily, thousands of artful and inflammatory publications, must
make in time a deep impression on the section of the Union where
they freely circulate, and are mainly designed to have effect. The
well-informed and thoughtful hold them in contempt, but the young,
the inexperienced, the ignorant, and thoughtless, will receive the
poison."

Source: William Lloyd Garrison, "Annual Report of the Board of Managers
of the Massachusetts Anti-Slavery Society, 1837."

Lydia Maria Childs, A Northern Abolitionist, Scolds Fellow Yankees Who Benefit from Slavery (1839)

Lydia Maria Child was an established novelist before marrying David Lee Child and beginning a career as an abolitionist writer. Unlike William Lloyd Garrison or Theodore Dwight Weld, she wrote calm, rational arguments against slavery designed to appeal to the intellect more than the emotions. In her "Anti-Slavery Catechism," she posed hypothetical questions of the kind that proslavery apologists typically asked when confronting abolitionists. In the following passage, she poses the question: if the slave system is as bad as abolitionists make it out to be, why are so many southerners unwilling to give it up? Her answer: partly because so many northerners are tacitly supporting it.

"At the North, the apologists of slavery are numerous and virulent, because their *interests* are closely intertwined with the pernicious system. Inquire into the private history of many of the men, who have called meetings against the abolitionists—you will find that some manufacture negro cloths for the South—some have sons who sell these cloths—some have daughters married to slave-holders—some have plantations and slaves mortgaged to them—some have ships employed in Southern commerce—and some candidates for political offices would bow until their back-bones were broken, to obtain or preserve Southern influence. The Southerners understand all this perfectly well and despise our servility, even while they condescend to make use of it."

Source: Lydia Maria Child, "Anti-Slavery Catechism." Newburyport, MA, 1839.

Theodore Dwight Weld, Abolitionists Make a Strong Case Against Slavery (1839)

Theodore Dwight Weld was an evangelical lecturer and writer for the American Anti-Slavery Society. Although not as famous as William Lloyd Garrison, he may have been more influential than Garrison in making converts to abolitionism. His 1839 compilation and publication of newspaper advertisements of slave holders looking for runaway slaves called American Slavery As It Is:

Testimony of a Thousand Witnesses *gave abolitionists more ammu-
nition with which to fight slavery than they had ever had before. It
also convinced many nominal opponents of slavery in the North to
join the abolition movement. In the following excerpts, Weld prefa-
ces his list of examples of "Punishments" for slaves who ran away,
which include floggings, branding, maiming, and gunshot
wounds, with an explanation of his research methods.*

"The slaves are terribly lacerated with whips, paddles, &c.; red
pepper and salt are rubbed into their mangled flesh; hot brine and
turpentine are poured into their gashes; and innumerable other
tortures are inflicted upon them.

"We will in the first place, prove by a cloud of witnesses, that the
slaves are whipped with such an inhuman severity, as to lacerate
and mangle their flesh in the most shocking manner, leaving
permanent scars and ridges; after establishing this, we will present
a mass of testimony, concerning a great variety of other tortures.
The testimony, for the most part, will be that of the slaveholders
themselves, and in their own chosen words. A large portion of it will
be taken from the advertisements, which they have published in
their own newspapers, describing by the scars on their bodies made
by the whip, their own runaway slaves.

. . .

"The slaves are often branded with hot irons, pursued with firearms
and *shot*, hunted with dogs and torn by them, shockingly maimed
with knives, dirks, &c; have their ears cut off, their eyes knocked
out, their bones dislocated and broken with bludgeons, their fingers
and toes cut off, their faces and other parts of their persons
disfigured with scars and gashes, *besides* those made with the lash."

Source: Excerpts from Theodore D. Weld, et al., *American Slavery As It
Is: Testimony of a Thousand Witnesses.* 1839; reprint. New York: Arno
Press, 1969.

James G. Birney, Abolitionists Launch Into
National Politics (1840)

*In 1840, the abolition movement suffered its great schism when the
Garrisonians and the New Yorkers disagreed over the women's*

rights question and over whether they should form a political party and compete in national elections. The New Yorkers broke from the American Anti-Slavery Society and formed a new organization called the American and Foreign Anti-Slavery Society, which was generally not as radical in its rhetoric or as unorthodox in its religious and social views. It chose instead to enter the political arena to compete with the Democrat and Whig Parties by creating the Liberty Party. It chose as its presidential candidate James G. Birney, a former Alabama slave holder. Below are excerpts from Birney's acceptance speech, which elucidate the raison d'etre *of the party.*

"So far as the Presidential question is concerned, this is the lamentable presentation made before the world;—of a Republic, professing in the most solemn manner, before the nations, that all men are created equal—that they are equally entitled to liberty and to the pursuit of happiness—having two candidates for her highest office—citizens of the free States—pledging their honor not themselves to disturb, and the official power with which they seek to be clothed, not to permit the National Legislature to disturb a system which wrests from ONE-SIXTH of our native countrymen their personal liberty—robs them of the rewards of their labor—scoffs at *their* right to pursuit of happiness, and sells them as beasts in the market. . . .

. . .

"The conclusion of the whole matter is, that, as a people, we are trying an experiment as unphilosophical in theory as it has been, and ever will be, found impossible in practice: to make a harmonious whole out of parts that are, in principle and essence, discordant. It is in vain to think of a sincere union between the North and the South, if the first remains true to her republican principles and habits, and the latter persist in her slaveholding despotism. They are incapable, from their natures, of being made *one.* They can no more be welded together into one body of uniform strength and consistency, than clay and brass. They may, it is true be pressed together and made to cohere by extraneous appliances; and the line of contact may be daubed over and varnished and concealed; but the first shock will make them fall asunder and disclose the fact, that there never was any real incorporation of the substance. A huge oligarchy, as the South is, made up of a multitude of petty despotisms, acting on the principle that men are *not* created equal—that a favored *few* are born, ready booted and spurred, to leap into the saddles which the backs of the *many* are furnished by nature—such a government, I say, when brought by circumstances into close juxtaposition and incessant intercourse with republics acting on principles diametrically opposite, must soon be brought to modify and eventually to relinquish its principles and practices,—or *vice versa*, the republics must undergo a similar change, and assimilate themselves to the practices of the despotisms. One or the other must, in the end, gain the entire ascendancy."

Source: Excerpts from Dwight L. Dumond, ed., *Letters of James Gillespie Birney, 1831–1857*. New York: D. Appleton-Century, 1939.

Solomon Northup, An Eyewitness Account of How Slave Auctions Affect Black Families (1853)

According to his memoir, Solomon Northup was born a free black in upstate New York and became a family man, a working man, and a musician. In 1841, two white con artists heard him playing his violin and talked him into traveling with them to Washington, D.C., where he could make a lot of money by joining the circus as a fiddler. In Washington, he was captured and sold into slavery for the next 12 years. His family, working with a New York attorney, finally found him in Louisiana and rescued him. He wrote his memoir and began a new life as an abolitionist. In this excerpt, he illustrates with great clarity one of the most disturbing aspects of slavery—the breaking up of families at slaves auctions—and thus one of the main reasons that abolitionism was necessary.

" . . . a number of sales were made. David and Caroline were purchased together by a Natchez planter. They left us, grinning broadly, and in a most happy state of mind, caused by the fact of their not being separated. Sethe was sold to a planter of Baton Rouge. . . .

"The same man also purchased Randall . . . All the time the trade was going on, Eliza was crying aloud, and wringing her hands. She besought the man not to buy him, unless he also bought herself and Emily. She promised, in that case to be the most faithful slave that ever lived. The man answered that he could not afford it, and then Eliza burst into a paroxysm of grief, weeping plaintively. Freeman turned round to her, savagely, with his whip in his uplifted hand, ordering her to stop her noise, or he would flog her. He would not have such work—such sniveling; and unless she ceased that minute, he would take her to the yard and give her a hundred lashes. Yes, he would take the nonsense out of her pretty quick—if he didn't, might he be d—d.

"Eliza shrunk before him, and tried to wipe away her tears, but it was all in vain. She wanted to be with her children, she said, the little time she had to live. All the frowns and threats of Freeman, could not wholly silence the afflicted mother. She kept on begging and beseeching them, most piteously, not to separate the three. Over and over again she told them how she loved her boy. A great many times she repeated her former promises—how very faithful and obedient she would be; how hard she would labor day and night, to the last moment of her life, if he would only buy them all together. But it was of no avail; the man could not afford it. The bargain was agreed upon and Randall must go alone. Then Eliza ran to him; embraced him passionately; kissed him again and again; told him to remember her—all the while her tears falling in the boy's face like rain.

"Freeman damned her, calling her a blubbering, bawling wench, and ordered her to go to her place, and behave herself, and be somebody. He swore he wouldn't stand such stuff but a little longer. He would soon give her something to cry about, if she was not mighty careful, and that she might depend upon.

"The planter from Baton Rouge, with his new purchase, was ready to depart.

"Don't cry, mama. I will be a good boy. Don't cry,' said Randall, looking back, as they passed out of the door.
"What has become of the lad, God knows. It was a mournful scene indeed. I would have cried myself if I had dared."

Source: Excerpt from Solomon Northup, *Twelve Years a Slave: Narrative of Solomon Northup*. Auburn, NY: Derby & Miller, 1853.

Henry Highland Garnet, The Most Radical
Solution to the Slavery Problem (1843)

In August 1843, the National Convention of Colored Citizens assembled in Buffalo, New York. Henry Highland Garnet, an escaped slave who had settled in New York City and trained for the ministry, gave the most memorable speech, urging his brethren in bondage in the South to rise up and take their freedom by force. Harkening back to David Walker's Appeal, *his militant message inspired radical abolitionists such as John Brown, garnered opposition from nonviolent activists such as Frederick Douglass, and struck fear and anger in the hearts of proslavery southerners. It illustrates with gripping effectiveness why abolitionism was such a complex movement; various abolition- ists had starkly different ideas about how to go about the work of ending slavery.*

"Brethren and Fellow Citizens,

"Your brethren of the North, East, and West have been accustomed to meet together in National Conventions, to sympathize with each other, and to weep over your unhappy condition. In these meetings we have addressed all classes of the free, but we have never, until this time, sent a word of consolation and advice to you. . . .

. . .

"Brethren, it is as wrong for your lordly oppressors to keep you in slavery, as it was for the man thief to steal our ancestors from the coast of Africa. You should therefore now use the same manner of resistance, as would have been just in our ancestors when the bloody foot-prints of the first remorseless soul-thief was placed upon the shores of our fatherland. . . .

"Brethren, the time has come when you must act for yourselves. It is an old and true saying that, 'if hereditary bondmen would be free, they must themselves strike the blow.' You can plead your own cause, and do the work of emancipation better than any others. . . .

. . .

"It is in your power so to torment the God-cursed slaveholders that they will be glad to let you go free. If the scale was turned, and black men were the masters and white men the slaves, every destructive agent and element would be employed to lay the oppressor low. Danger and death would hang over their heads day and night. Yes, the tyrants would meet with plagues more terrible than those of Pharaoh. But you are a patient people. You act as though you were made for the special use of these devils. You act as though your daughters were born to pamper the lusts of your masters and overseers. And worse than all, you tamely submit while your lords tear your wives from your embraces and defile them before your eyes. In the name of God, we ask, are you men? Where is the blood of your fathers? . . . .

"Let your motto be resistance! *Resistance!* Resistance! . . ."

Source: Excerpts from Henry Highland Garnet, *Walker's Appeal: With a Brief Sketch of His Life by Henry Highland Garnet: And Also Garnet's Address to the Slaves of the United States of America.* New York: J.H. Tobitt, 1848.

Frederick Douglass, Independence Day—National Holiday or Merely White American Holiday? (1852)

The most renowned black abolitionist was Frederick Douglass, a slave who escaped from Maryland, joined up with William Lloyd Garrison and the American Anti-Slavery Society, traveled the abolitionist lecture circuit, published his autobiography, and edited the North Star *newspaper. Noted for his striking appearance, his silver tongue, his command of the English language, his tragic life story, his level head, and his even temperament, he could mesmerize an audience. Here in an address at Rochester, New York, on July 5, 1852, he dismantled the national day of celebration called Independence Day. To slaves, he complained, there was nothing to celebrate.*

"Fellow-citizens, pardon me, allow me to ask, why am I called upon to speak here to-day? What have I, or those I represent, to do with your national independence? Are the great principles of political freedom and of natural justice, embodied in that Declaration of Independence, extended to us? . . .

. . .

"Your high independence only reveals the immeasurable distance between us. The blessings in which you, this day, rejoice, are not enjoyed in common. The rich inheritance of justice, liberty, prosperity and independence, bequeathed by your fathers, is shared by you, not by me. The sunlight that brought light and healing to you, has brought stripes and death to me. This Fourth [of] July is *yours*, not *mine. You* may rejoice, *I* must mourn. . . .

. . .

"Standing with God and the crushed and bleeding slave on this occasion, I will, in the name of humanity which is outraged, in the name of liberty which is fettered, in the name of the constitution and the Bible, which are disregarded and trampled upon, dare to call in question and to denounce, with all the emphasis I can command, everything that serves to perpetuate slavery—the great sin and shame of America! . . .

. . .

"What to the slave is your 4th of July? I answer: a day that reveals to him, more than all other days in the year, the gross injustice and cruelty to which he is the constant victim. To him, your celebration is a sham; your boasted liberty, an unholy license; your national greatness, swelling vanity; your sounds of rejoicing are empty and heartless; your denunciation of tyrants, brass fronted impudence; your shouts of liberty and equality, hollow mockery; your prayers and hymns, your sermons and thanksgivings, with all your religious parade, and solemnity, are, to him, mere bombast, fraud, deception, impiety, and hypocrisy—a thin veil to cover up crimes which would disgrace a nation of savages. There is not a nation on the earth guilty of practices more shocking and bloody than are the people of the United States, at this very hour. . . ."

Source: Excerpts from Frederick Douglass, "What to the Slave Is the Fourth of July?" quoted in Philip S. Foner, ed., *The Life and Writings of*

Frederick Douglass, vol. II, Pre-Civil War Decade, 1850–1860. New York: International Publishers, 1950.

Frederick Douglass, Assessing the Various Abolition Organizations (1855)

As a former slave, Douglass stood in a good position to judge the strategies and effectiveness of the four main arms of the abolition movement, all of which were run by white men with noble intentions. He identifies the American Anti-Slavery Society as the "Garrisonian" society and the American and Foreign Anti-Slavery Society as the "Anti-Garrisonian" society. Likewise, he relabels the Liberty Party as the "Gerrit Smith School of Abolitionists" and the Free Soil Party as the "Political Abolitionists." Here, in a speech given in Rochester, New York, in 1855, he finds fault with three of these and throws his support behind the fourth.

" . . . I propose to speak of the different anti-slavery sects and parties, and to give my view of them briefly. There are four principal divisions.

. . .

"I shall consider, first, the Garrisonian Anti-Slavery Society. . . . This society is the oldest of modern Anti-Slavery Societies. It has, strictly speaking, two weekly papers or organs—employs five or six lecturers—and holds numerous public meetings for dissemination of its views. Its peculiar and distinctive feature is, its doctrine of *'no union with slaveholders'*. . . . [which] carried out, dissolves the Union, and leaves the slaves and masters to fight their own battles, in their own way. This I hold to be an abandonment of the great idea with which that Society was started. It started to free the slaves. It ends by leaving the slave to free himself.

. . .

" . . . The American and Foreign Anti-Slavery Society has not yet departed from the original ground, but stands where the American Anti-Slavery Society stood at the beginning. The energies of this association are mainly directed to the revival of anti-slavery in the

Church. It is active in the collection, and in the circulation of facts, exposing the character of slavery. . . . It does not aim to abolish the Union, but aims to avail itself of the means afforded by the Union to abolish slavery. . . . Nevertheless I am somewhat against this Society. . . . It has almost dropped the main and most potent weapon with which slavery is to be assailed and overthrown, and that is speech. At this moment . . . [it] has not a single lecturing agent in the field.

"The next recognized anti-slavery body is the Free Soil party . . . .Its motto is " *Slavery Local—Liberty National.*" The objection to this movement is . . . .It leaves the slaves in his [*sic*] fetters.

"The fourth division . . . is, the " *Liberty Party*"—a small body of citizens, chiefly in the State of New York, but having sympathizers all over the North. It is the radical, and to my thinking, the *only* abolition organization in the country, except a few local associations. It makes a clean sweep of slavery everywhere. It denies that slavery is, or *can* be legalized. It denies that the Constitution of the United States is a pro-slavery instrument, and asserts the power and duty of the Federal Government to abolish slavery in every State in the Union."

Source: Excerpts from "Frederick Douglass Reviews the Progress of Abolition (1855)," quoted in John L. Thomas, ed., *Slavery Attacked: The Abolitionist Crusade.* Englewood Cliffs, NJ: Prentice Hall, 1965.

Wendell Phillips, A Garrisonian, Defends Garrisonianism (1853)

Wendell Phillips was the most important disciple of William Lloyd Garrison. Widely considered the best orator of all the abolitionists, he defended Garrison and his American Anti-Slavery Society against denunciations, such as the one cited in the preceding Frederick Douglass speech. Here, before a mostly friendly audience in Boston in 1853, he points out that without Garrison, great political leaders such as John Quincy Adams, Charles Sumner, Salmon Chase, and Joshua Giddings may have never joined the ranks of the abolitionists.

" . . . Who converted these men and their distinguished associates?. . . . They were all converted by the 'hot,' 'reckless,' 'ranting,' 'bigoted,' 'fanatic' Garrison. . . . Do not criticize too much the agency by which such men were converted. That blade has a double edge. Our reckless course, our empty rant, our fanaticism, has made Abolitionists of some of the best and ablest men in the land. We are inclined to go on, and see if even with such poor tools we cannot make some more. . . .

. . .

"Caution is not always good policy in a cause like ours.

. . .

" . . . [I]n critical times, when a wrong step entails most disastrous consequences, to 'mean well' is not enough. Sincerity is no shield for any man from the criticism of his fellow-laborers. . . .

"Every thoughtful and unprejudiced mind must see that such an evil as slavery will yield only to the most radical treatment. If you consider the work we have to do, you will not think us needlessly aggressive . . .

. . . Slavery has been made the question of this generation. To startle the South to madness, so that every step she takes, in her blindness, is one step more toward ruin, is much. This we have done . . . Our question is . . . [i]f our agitation has not been wisely planned and conducted, explain for us the history of the last twenty years! . . ."

Source: Excerpts from Wendell Phillips, *Speeches, Lectures, and Letters.* Boston: Lothrop Lee & Shepard, 1863.

Williams Wells Brown, Abolitionists Must Not Rest Even After the Emancipation Proclamation (1864)

Abolitionists saw the Emancipation Proclamation and preliminary cases in which slaves were liberated not as signs of victory in the war against slavery but merely as important steps in that direction. At the New England Anti-Slavery Convention in Boston in May 1864, William Wells Brown, an escaped slave from Kentucky turned abolitionist, expressed fear that slavery might survive even if the Confederacy were destroyed.

"Slavery has received a severe, it may be a fatal blow. Yet the colored man has everything to fear. Even when Grant's army shall be successful, we, the colored people, will be in danger. The advantages we have so far received have come as much through Jeff. Davis as through President Lincoln. The war was begun with the purpose of restoring the nation as it was, and leaving the black man where he was. Now the time has come when you must recognize the black man as on the same footing with the white man. If not, the mission of this war is not ended, and we must have yet more disasters to scourge us into the right way."

Source: Quoted in William Edward Farrison, *William Wells Brown: Author and Reformer.* Chicago: University of Chicago Press, 1969.

Glossary

Abolition Movement   Also known as the antislavery movement, it was an organized sociopolitical campaign to end slavery in the United States, lasting roughly from 1829 to 1865. Before the 1840s, it was spearheaded by private citizens, such as William Lloyd Garrison and Arthur and Lewis Tappan, rather than political leaders or a government. Thereafter, it became an increasingly political movement.

Abolitionism   The ideology of the abolition movement. It opposed the continuation of slavery in the United States, mainly based on the Christian belief that slave holding and slave trading are sins, the Natural Law principle of the equality of all people, or both.

Abolitionists   The public opponents of slavery and leaders of the abolition movement. A few scattered individuals in the United States could be called abolitionists before the 1830s, most of whom were Pennsylvania Quakers. Their numbers swelled throughout the northern states among various denominations in and after the 1830s, largely as a result of the work of William Lloyd Garrison and of political developments involving the American West.

Apologist   One who makes a formal defense of a particular ideology or dogma, whether religious, philosophical, or political. It does not mean one who regrets what he or she believes or feels on the points he or she is defending. Herein, the apologists are defined as proslavery ideologues and political leaders who gave the best explanations for their defense of slavery. Depending on what time period in history each one lived, some were also members of the "slavocracy" or the "Fire-Eaters" or were identified as part of the "slave power" in America.

Barnburners   New York antislavery Democrats who, in the late 1840s, broke from the national Democrat Party to help form the new Free Soil Party.

Chattel   (rhymes with "cattle") Personal property other than real estate, which is recognized by law. Refers to permanent slaves rather than indentured servants and to how slave holders had absolute control over them and could do with them as they pleased.

Colonization   The practice of sending freed slaves to a foreign land, usually Africa, for relocation. It generally resulted from slave holders not wanting their former slaves to become their free neighbors or from the fear that free blacks would be treated worse in society than slaves were treated. Its most notable proponent was the American Colonization Society.

Comity   The practice of one state government respecting the laws of another state government. In terms of slavery, it generally meant that free states were expected to respect the laws of slave states and cooperate with them in catching runaway slaves.

Doughface   A nickname for northern politicians who sided with southerners on the slavery issue, particularly in the 1850s. Mainly it was applied to Democrats, such as Presidents Franklin Pierce and James Buchanan. It also described most common folks in the North, a majority of whom were either opposed to abolition or simply apathetic about slavery.

Emancipation   The process of freeing or liberating a person or group from slavery. Usually used in the context of a government action. It came in two forms—compensated and uncompensated emancipation. The former called for the U.S. government to pay slave holders the value of their loss if a law were passed emancipating the slaves. The latter did not.

Fire-Eaters   Southern leaders who, from 1850 to 1861, called for the southern states to secede from the Union because of growing abolitionist sentiment in the North. The term was first applied to the secessionists at the Nashville Convention of 1850 and later to the secessionists who led in forming the Confederate States of America in 1861. They were all part of the collective "slave power," as the abolitionist Henry Wilson termed the proslavery leaders in the U.S. government.

Gradualism   A particular abolition strategy that called for slaves to be set free little by little rather than all at once to lessen the impact on the socioeconomic structure of the country. It was most popular before the 1830s. It is synonymous with *gradual emancipation.*

Immediatism   A particular abolition strategy that called for all slaves to be set free at once, regardless of any socioeconomic disruption that might occur. It was pioneered in the United States by William Lloyd Garrison and the American Anti-Slavery Society in and after the 1830s.

Know-Nothing Party   Beginning in 1849 in New York as a secret, fraternal organization that opposed the growth of Catholicism and the increase of immigration from non-Protestant Christian countries, it evolved into a national political party that achieved the height of its influence in the northeastern United States from 1854 to 1856. Officially called the American Party, it distracted many northern voters and political leaders from focusing on abolitionism in the 1850s.

Manumission   The practice of slave holders voluntarily freeing their slaves. It generally provided the only method by which slaves in southern states were freed before the Civil War. It was a prerequisite for colonization.

Mendicant   A vagabond or derelict; a pauper or person unable to provide for himself or his family and thus lived off of public welfare or private charity. In terms of slavery, it refers to the fear that some whites had that freeing the slaves would produce millions of beggars and thieves.

Miscegenation   A term deriving from Latin that means race mixing or interbreeding, particularly between blacks and whites. It was coined as part of a hoax by Democrats in New York who wanted to portray Republicans during the Civil War as being in favor of racial mixing, which the vast majority Americans opposed.

Moral Suasion   A term dating back hundreds of years that originated in England which American abolitionists adopted to explain their method of trying to make converts in the early 1800s. It was a strategy geared toward preaching to slave holders, urging them to repent of the sin of slave holding, lest God judge them individually and the United States as a whole. It also incorporated rational intellectual arguments in with theology that worked upon the individual conscience of each slave holder.

Mulatto   A term deriving from the root word "mule," which described racially mixed Americans, most of whom were slaves. Any individual racial composition other than supposedly pure white would qualify a person as a mulatto in the United States.

Peculiar Institution   A nickname given to the form of slavery that had arisen in, and that was therefore unique or "peculiar" to, the American South in the early 1800s. The term was coined by John C. Calhoun, a senator from South Carolina, in 1829, and used by a former slave named Peter Randolph in his memoir in 1855. It only came into common usage as a euphemism for slavery in the mid-twentieth century with the publication of Kenneth Stampp's book of the same name.

Popular Sovereignty   A political ideology that says local residents or voters should have the final decision over all local government matters. It predates the founding of the United States but was first applied here in the late 1840s. Made famous by Democrats Lewis Cass of Michigan and Stephen A. Douglas of Illinois, it was used to try to solve the constant bickering between the North and South over whether new states should be allowed to have slavery or not by allowing voters in each western territory to decide the issue for themselves. It represented a marked departure from the traditional method in which Congress determined whether a new state or territory would be free or slave.

Redention   A term meaning for fugitive slaves captured in the North to be legally extradited and physically returned to their state of origin in the South.

Slavocracy   A nickname that John Quincy Adams gave to the leading proslavery apologists in the 1840s. It refers to the South's landed aristocracy that built its wealth, power, and prestige on the back of slave labor. Sometimes referred to as the "slave power" in America, many of this group's members were later called "Fire-Eaters."

Underground Railroad   A name given to the system comprising the network of abolitionists and their methods of and routes for helping slaves escape from southern states to the northern United States or Canada. It was "underground" in the sense that it operated illegally and therefore had to be kept secret. It was a "railroad" in that it had certain, special transportation routes, which included "stations" (usually private homes or churches of abolitionists that took in fugitives and hid them by day, sending them on to the next station by night) and "conductors" (organizers of the network and sometimes hands-on helpers of fugitives). Although there were individual conductors and scattered stations before the 1840s, the term became popular in and after the 1840s and was probably coined by a Maryland conductor named Charles Turner Torrey.

Annotated Bibliography

There are currently more than 100 books in print that are devoted solely to the abolition movement. Hundreds more cover individual abolitionists or some aspect of the movement. There are many aspects—women, blacks, white southern dissidents, Quakers, other religious groups, political parties, the Underground Railroad, and the West, just to name a few. For abolitionism to make sense, the reader must first know some basic facts about the institution of slavery and the slave trade, and hundreds of books touch on all different aspects of those issues as well.

Books

Abzug, Robert H. *Passionate Liberator: Theodore Dwight Weld and the Dilemma of Reform.* New York: Oxford University Press, 1980.

A revision or addition to the earlier biography of Weld by Benjamin Thomas. A psychohistory that focuses on the factors that led Weld to abandon his public life as an abolitionist.

American Social History Project. *Who Built America? Working People and the Nation's History, Volume I: To 1877.* 3rd ed. Boston: Bedford/St. Martin's, 2008.

Survey of all American social and racial history. Part Two: "Free Labor and Slavery, 1790–1850" provides an excellent overview of the dichotomy of the North and South in terms of labor. Contains primary documents and illustrations.

Andrews, William L., and William S. McFeely, eds. *Narrative of the Life of Frederick Douglass, An American Slave, Written by Himself.* New York: W. W. Norton & Company, 1997.

One of several edited editions of Douglass's autobiography, this one contains sections called "Contexts" and "Criticisms," which are historiography and literary criticism.

Aptheker, Herbert. *American Negro Slave Revolts*. New York: International Publishers, 1963 ed.

A long, scholarly, pioneering study of the topic by one of the giants in the field of black history in the generation before it became fashionable.

Aptheker, Herbert. *Negro Slave Revolts in the United States*. New York: International Publishers, 1939.

A very brief, undocumented, but important book. One of the first revisionist histories written that challenged the notion that slave holders were mostly kind to their slaves.

Aptheker, Herbert. *"One Continual Cry": David Walker's* Appeal to the Colored Citizens of the World *(1829–1830)—Its Setting & Its Meaning*. New York: Humanities Press, 1965.

A mostly historiographical look at the impact of Walker's *Appeal* in both his contemporary times and in history.

Archer, Jules. *Angry Abolitionist: William Lloyd Garrison*. New York: Julian Messner, 1969.

A brief biography written for students and lay people rather than scholars.

Bailey, Hugh. *Hinton Rowan Helper: Abolitionist and Racist*. Tuscaloosa: University of Alabama Press, 1965.

Standard biography of this unique southern enigma who was, as the title implies, strongly antislavery and staunchly racist at the same time.

Baker, George E. *The Works of William H. Seward*. New York: Redfield, 1853.

Three-volume first-hand published papers of one of the leading political abolitionists of the 1850s and 1860s.

Baker, Houston A., Jr., ed. *Narrative of the Life of Frederick Douglass, an American Slave, Written by Himself.* New York: Penguin Books, 1982 ed.

Primary source with an editorial introduction that places Douglass's memoir in historical perspective.

Barnes, Gilbert Hobbs. *The Antislavery Impulse, 1830–1844.* New York: D. Appleton-Century, 1933.

One of the first standard treatments of abolitionism by a professional historian in the generation after the abolitionists died off.

Bartlett, Ruhl J. *John C. Fremont and the Republican Party.* New York: Da Capo Press, 1970.

A brief but scholarly biography of the enigmatic Fremont that portrays him as a moderate antislavery man.

Berlin, Ira. *Many Thousands Gone: The First Two Centuries of Slavery in North America.* Cambridge, MA: The Belknap Press, 1998.

A long, scholarly, broad, and sweeping account of slavery in the Colonial Era.

Berwanger, Eugene H. *The Frontier Against Slavery: Western Anti-Negro Prejudice and the Slavery Extension Controversy.* Urbana, IL: University of Illinois Press, 1967.

Argues, as the title implies, that western frontier whites were opposed to slavery not because they were abolitionists but because they did not want blacks moving into their territories and states.

Bilotta, James D. *Race and the Rise of the Republican Party, 1848–1865.* New York: Peter Lang, 1992.

Long, scholarly, revisionist assessment of the Free Soilers and founding fathers of the Republican Party as racists.

Blassingame, John W., ed. *The Frederick Douglass Papers.* New Haven, CT: Yale University Press, 1979.

The most thorough treatment of Douglass available. Contains five thick volumes arranged chronologically, each of which includes an editorial introduction and its own subchronology.

Bordewich, Fergus M. *Bound for Canaan: The Underground Railroad and the War for the Soul of America*. New York: Amistad, 2005.

A long, narrative history written without classic footnotes but rather with modern journalistic endnotes. Has an excellent glossy illustration spread.

Borkin, Benjamin A., ed. *Lay My Burden Down: A Folk History of Slavery*. Chicago: University of Chicago Press, 1945.

A collection of slave narratives compiled and edited in the pre–civil rights movement era before sensitivity to the feelings of blacks was as much a concern as it has been in later times when discussing slavery.

Bridges, Kenneth, ed. *Freedom in America*. Upper Saddle River, NJ: Pearson, 2008.

A collection of primary documents. Contains selections by Abraham Lincoln, Frederick Douglass, Sojourner Truth, Samuel Sewall, Phyllis Wheatley, and others on slavery and abolition.

Browne, Stephen Howard. *Angelina Grimke: Rhetoric, Identity, and the Radical Imagination*. East Lansing, MI: Michigan State University Press, 1999.

A psychohistory that is written for scholars familiar with the jargon in this field. Not recommended for lay people or beginner students.

Budney, Stephen P. *William Jay: Abolitionist and Anticolonialist*. Westport, CT: Praeger, 2005.

A brief but scholarly biography. Jay was an important but largely forgotten New York abolitionist. The son of the Founding Father John Jay, he was quiet and moderate in his approach to abolitionism, which kept him out of the spotlight that other abolitionists, such as William Lloyd Garrison, craved.

Burin, Eric. *Slavery and the Peculiar Solution: A History of the American Colonization Society*. Gainesville, FL: University Press of Florida, 2005.

A brief but scholarly survey of the American Colonization Society's history that emphasizes its role in the antebellum period.

Burrow, Rufus, Jr. *God and Human Responsibility: David Walker and Ethical Prophecy.* Macon, GA: Mercer University Press, 2003.

A study in self-described "prophetic ethics" that treats the *Appeal* as a theological treatise on social justice in the same vein as Old Testament prophetic books.

Cable, Mary. *Black Odyssey: The Case of the Slave Ship* Amistad. New York: Viking, 1971.

A brief, undocumented primer on the topic. Contains an important appendix of names and African pronunciations of the participants in the revolt along with silhouette portraits and a mini biography of each.

Cain, William E., ed. *William Lloyd Garrison and the Fight Against Slavery: Selections from the* Liberator. New York: Bedford/ St. Martin's, 1994.

Contains a brief but thorough editorial introduction followed by 41 articles from the *Liberator* covering all phases of its publication from 1831 to 1865. Illustrations, chronology, and questions for students are also included.

Carnahan, Burrus M. *Act of Justice: Lincoln's Emancipation Proclamation and the Law of War.* Lexington, KY: University Press of Kentucky, 2007.

A brief but scholarly look at the legal issues surrounding the Emancipation Proclamation and how Lincoln's actions have application for modern presidents in times of war.

Carton, Eric. *Patriotic Treason: John Brown and the Soul of America.* New York: Free Press, 2006.

A sympathetic account that sees Brown as the heir of the patriotism that sparked the American Revolution and founded the United States. Documented with new journalistic style endnotes.

Catterall, Helen Tunnicliff and James Hayden, eds. *Judicial Cases Concerning American Slavery and the Negro.* Washington, D.C.: The Carnegie Institution, 1926–1937.

Five-volume set covering cases in England, Canada, and Jamaica, as well as cases in many states in the United States. Includes editorial explanations and actual primary document court rulings.

Commager, Henry Steele, ed. *Documents of American History*, 7th ed. New York: Appleton-Century-Crofts, 1963.

Large collection of primary documents covering all of American history. Useful for putting the abolition movement into the larger context of the times.

Curtain, Philip D. *The Atlantic Slave Trade: A Census*. Madison, WI: University of Wisconsin Press, 1969.

For many years the standard treatment of the victimization of the Africans by the slave trade.

DeCaro, Louis A., Jr. *"Fire from the Midst of You": A Religious Life of John Brown*. New York: New York University Press, 2002.

A scholarly and sympathetic psychohistory of Brown, focusing on his religious motivations.

Dillon, Merton L. *The Abolitionists: The Growth of a Dissenting Minority*. DeKalb, IL: Northern Illinois University Press, 1974.

A thorough, scholarly account of the movement from the American Revolution to Reconstruction. A good starting point for students and lay readers.

Dillon, Merton L. *Slavery Attacked: Southern Slaves and the Allies, 1619–1865*. Baton Rouge, LA: Louisiana State University Press, 1990.

Not to be confused with John L. Thomas's book of the same name, this book is a scholarly but not overly esoteric survey of slavery and the abolition movement in the United States from beginning to end.

Donnan, Elizabeth. *Documents Illustrative of the History of the Slave Trade to America*. New York: Octagon Books, 1965.

Four-volume set containing more than 1,100 primary documents, running from 1441 to 1800 and covering New England and the South and the border colonies and states separately.

Du Bois, W. E. B. *John Brown: A Biography*. 1909; reprint. Armonk, NY: M.E. Sharpe, 1997.

A classic that has been updated with an introduction and primary documents by John David Smith.

Dumond, Dwight Lowell. *Antislavery: The Crusade for Freedom in America*. Ann Arbor, MI: University of Michigan Press, 1961.

Perhaps the best all-around treatment of the abolition movement, although too adoring of abolitionists. Very detailed. Omits John Brown and the Civil War.

Dumond, Dwight Lowell, ed. *Letters of James Gillespie Birney, 1831–1857*. New York: D. Appleton-Century, 1938.

A two-volume set that contains some 34 articles and speeches written by Birney and about 500 letters written by or to him.

Earle, Jonathan H. *Jacksonian Antislavery and the Politics of Free Soil, 1824–1854*. Chapel Hill: University of North Carolina Press, 2004.

A brief but scholarly account with helpful illustrations. Focuses on the antislavery dissidents within a mostly proslavery party.

Earle, Jonathan H. *John Brown's Raid on Harper's Ferry: A Brief History with Documents*. Boston: Bedford/St. Martin's, 2008.

Short, good mini biography with primary source documents. Recommended for students.

Elliott, E. N., ed. *Cotton Is King, and Pro-Slavery Arguments* . . . Augusta, GA: Pritchard, Abbott & Loomis, 1860.

The definitive compendium of proslavery books and essays. Authors include David Christy, Albert Taylor Bledsoe, Thornton Stringfellow, Chancellor Harper, J. H. Hammond, Charles Hodge, and Samuel Cartwright. Also includes complete texts of the Dred Scott decision and the Fugitive Slave Act of 1850.

Ericson, David F. *The Debate over Slavery: Antislavery and Pro-slavery Liberalism in Antebellum America*. New York: New York University Press, 2000.

Argues that proslavery thought was actually part of the American tradition of liberalism rather than a conservative (which Ericson calls "illiberal" or "non-liberal") philosophy. Fascinating but deep. Recommended for scholars rather than lay readers or beginner students.

Etcheson, Nicole. *Bleeding Kansas: Contested Liberty in the Civil War Era*. Lawrence, KS: University Press of Kansas, 2004.

A scholarly political history that follows the saga of Kansas from its territorial period in the 1850s through the Exoduster movement of the 1870s.

Fanuzzi, Robert. *Abolition's Public Sphere*. Minneapolis: University of Minnesota Press, 2003.

Focuses mostly on William Lloyd Garrison, Frederick Douglass, and Henry David Thoreau and their efforts to publicize the abolition movement by getting it out of the churches and into the public forum (but not into politics). Contains erudite jargon. Recommended for scholars rather than lay readers or beginner students.

Fehrenbacher, Don E. *The Dred Scott Case: Its Significance in American Law and Politics*. New York: Oxford University Press, 1978.

Scholarly and long, as most of Fehrenbacher's books are, made for specialists and teachers more so than students or lay readers.

Fehrenbacher, Don E. and Ward M. McAfee. *The Slaveholding Republic: An Account of the United States Government's Relations to Slavery*. New York: Oxford University Press, 2001.

A long, scholarly look at the U.S. Constitution and whether it was proslavery, antislavery, or neutral. It argues the neutral position, thus showing that abolitionists and proslavery southerners as a whole were both extremists in their constitutional interpretations.

Ferrell, Claudine L. *The Abolitionist Movement*. Westport, CT: Greenwood Press, 2005.

An excellent starting point for students. A brief account written for lay readers, not scholars. Contains primary documents and an annotated bibliography with more than 200 illustrations.

Filler, Louis. *The Crusade Against Slavery, 1830–1860*. New York: Harper & Row, 1960.

Sets the standard by which other books on abolitionism are judged.

Finkenbine, Roy E., ed. *Sources of the African American Past: Primary Sources in American History*. 2nd ed. New York: Pearson-Longman, 2004.

Has several primary source documents that help illuminate the abolition movement.

Foner, Philip S. *Life and Writings of Frederick Douglass*. New York: International Publishers, 1950.

A five-volume set that begins with a 100-page biography followed by a collection of Douglass's writings, speeches, and correspondence.

Ford, Lacy K. *Deliver Us from Evil: The Slavery Question in the Old South*. New York: Oxford University Press, 2009.

A long, scholarly look at the variety of attitudes about slavery among southern whites in the Early Republic and the beginning of the Jacksonian Era, showing the distinctions from state to state and region to region.

Franklin, John Hope and Alfred A. Moss, Jr. *From Slavery to Freedom: A History of African Americans*. 8th ed. Boston: McGraw-Hill, 2000.

Standard survey of all of black American history. Recommended as a primer for students.

Franklin, John Hope, Alfred A. Moss, Jr., and Loren Schweninger. *Runaway Slaves: Rebels on the Plantation*. New York: Oxford University Press, 1999.

A long, scholarly work covering all aspects of the fugitive slave issue in the 1800s. Contains appendices of primary sources and demographics of runaways.

Frederickson, George M., ed. *William Lloyd Garrison*. Englewood Cliffs, NJ: Prentice-Hall, 1968.

An important revisionist account that deemphasizes the importance of Garrison to the overall movement. Contains some of Garrison's writings that are exemplary of his work and looks at how some contemporaries viewed him at the time and how some historians have viewed him since.

Frothingham, Octavius Brooks. *Gerrit Smith: A Biography*. 1878; reprint. New York: Negro Universities Press, 1969.

First-hand, sympathetic account of the life of the wealthy upstate New York abolitionist.

Garrison, Wendell Phillips and Francis Jackson Garrison, eds. *William Lloyd Garrison, 1805–1879: The Story of His Life Told by His Children*. New York: Century, 1885–1889.

Primary and eyewitness accounts. Four volumes.

Gates, Henry Louis, Jr., ed. *Frederick Douglass: Autobiographies*. New York: The Library of America, 1994.

Contains all three of Douglass's autobiographies, a very detailed chronology of Douglass's entire life, and an editorial notes section explaining unclear statements or references.

Genovese, Eugene. *The Slaveholders' Dilemma: Freedom and Progress in Southern Conservative Thought, 1820–1860*. Columbia, SC: University of South Carolina Press, 1992.

Shows that some mostly forgotten proslavery and states' rights ideologues of the antebellum South were, contrary to popular misconception, world-class intellectuals who deserve to be studied rather than simply dismissed as wrong-headed racists.

George, James Z. *The Political History of Slavery in the United States*. 1915; reprint. New York: Negro Universities Press, 1969.

A 100-page treatise on slavery and abolition from a southern racist's perspective at the height of the era of white supremacy.

Goodman, Paul. *Of One Blood: Abolitionism and the Origins of Racial Equality*. Berkeley, CA: University of California Press, 1998.

Published posthumously, this book traces the history of the idea of racial equality from the founding of the United States during the Age of Enlightenment through its evolution among abolitionists in the 1830s.

Gougeon, Len and Joel Myerson, eds. *Emerson's Antislavery Writings*. New Haven, CT: Yale University Press, 1995.

Contains a brief but thorough editorial introduction to the life of the great New England Transcendentalist Ralph Waldo Emerson followed by selections from his addresses and speeches on slavery and abolition from 1838 to 1863.

Greenberg, Kenneth S. *Nat Turner: A Slave Rebellion in History and Memory*. New York: Oxford University Press, 2003.

A scholarly account of the Nat Turner rebellion and the historiography of the topic.

Greenberg, Kenneth S., ed. *The Confessions of Nat Turner and Related Documents*. Boston: St. Martin's, 1996.

A brief collection of primary documents from Turner, the governor of Virginia, the trial, and contemporary newspapers.

Griffler, Keith P. *Front Line of Freedom: African Americans and the Forging of the Underground Railroad in the Ohio Valley*. Lexington, KY: University Press of Kentucky, 2004.

A brief but scholarly account of efforts to help slaves escape from Kentucky to Ohio. Has excellent illustrations.

Hagedorn, Ann. *Beyond the River: The Untold Story of the Heroes of the Underground Railroad*. New York: Simon & Schuster, 2002.

A scholarly narrative that focuses mostly on John Rankin's role in the Underground Railroad in Ripley, Ohio.

Harrold, Stanley C., Jr. *The Rise of Aggressive Abolitionism: Addresses to the Slaves*. Lexington, KY: University Press of Kentucky, 2004.

A brief but scholarly look at three separate addresses given supposedly to the southern slaves as a whole by northern abolitionists

(William Lloyd Garrison, Gerrit Smith, and Henry Highland Garnet), which no slaves were present to hear.

Helper, Hinton Rowan. *The Impending Crisis of the South and How to Meet It.* New York: Burdick Brothers, 1857.

One of the seminal works of the abolition movement. Written by a southerner with strong antislavery views that were based on economic objections to slavery rather than religious or political ones. Criticized by Helper's biographer, Hugh Bailey, for its limitations, which he says were caused partly by the fact that Helper had never lived in the North and therefore had little understanding of the North's industrial economy and way of life.

Herbert, Hilary A. *The Abolition Crusade and Its Consequences.* New York: Charles Scribner's Sons, 1912.

A southern racist account from the post–Civil War generation that shows some of the complexities of abolitionism. Herbert was opposed to slavery, yet he fought for the Confederacy. He was strongly opposed to racial equality, but he served patriotically in the U.S. government after the war.

Herskovitz, Melville J. *The Myth of the Negro Past.* New York: Harper & Brothers, 1941.

A classic sociological study in the field of black history. Shows that African slaves had a rich cultural heritage that was transmitted to the United States.

Hildreth, Richard. *Despotism in America: An Inquiry Into the Nature, Results, and Legal Basis of the Slave-Holding System in the United States.* 1854; reprint. New York: Negro Universities Press, 1968.

Primary source. A long, scholarly, philosophical and political argument against slavery. Considers the U.S. government a grand experiment in democracy and egalitarianism that the South was deliberately rejecting and thwarting by maintaining the slave system.

Hinks, Peter P. *David Walker's* Appeal to the Colored Citizens of the World. University Park, PA: The Pennsylvania State University Press, 2000.

A brief but important addition to the literature on Walker's *Appeal*, which supplements Hinks' earlier work. A good starting point for students researching the topic.

Hinks, Peter P. *To Awaken My Afflicted Brethren: David Walker and the Problem of Antebellum Slave Resistance*. University Park, PA: The Pennsylvania State University Press, 1997.

Perhaps the definitive analysis of Walker and his *Appeal*. In depth and scholarly. Proves almost beyond a doubt that Walker was not murdered but died of natural causes.

Holzer, Harold and Sara Vaughn Gabbard, eds. *Lincoln and Freedom: Slavery, Emancipation, and the Thirteenth Amendment*. Carbondale, IL: Southern Illinois University Press, 2007.

A collection of 15 essays written by some of the most distinguished scholars in the field. Emphasizes Lincoln's signing of the 13th Amendment as an overlooked but important proof of his full conversion to a racial egalitarian by the end of the war.

Holzer, Harold, Edna Greene Medford, and Frank J. Williams, et al., eds. *The Emancipation Proclamation: Three Views [Social, Political, Iconographic]*. Baton Rouge, LA: Louisiana State University Press, 2006.

Looks at conflicting views of the Emancipation Proclamation as Lincoln's greatest achievement versus merely a desperate effort to win the war through racial propaganda.

Hosmer, William. *Slavery and the Church*. 1853; reprint. New York: Negro Universities Press, 1969.

Primary source. One of several polemics written during the abolition movement that argued that slavery was a sin and crime against humanity. Published in the 1850s after such arguments had lost their effectiveness.

Howard, Warren S. *American Slavers and Federal Law, 1837–1862*. Berkeley, CA: University of California Press, 1963.

A thorough, scholarly monograph proving the pervasiveness of the illegal slave trade during the years of the abolition movement. Shows that about 100 American ships were caught in the act of transporting slaves illegally in international waters over a 25-year span.

Hudson, J. Blaine. *Encyclopedia of the Underground Railroad.* Jefferson, NC: McFarland & Company, 2006.

An indispensible reference book for studying the Underground Railroad.

Huggins, Nathan Irvin. *Slave and Citizen: The Life of Frederick Douglass.* Boston: Little, Brown and Company, 1980.

A brief, undocumented biographical primer that makes a good starting point for students on this topic.

Jackson, Ruby T. and Walter T. McDonald. *Finding Freedom: The Untold Story of Joshua Glover, Runaway Slave.* Madison: Wisconsin Historical Society Press, 2007.

A brief but scholarly account of one of the notable events of the 1850s involving a runaway slave, the Fugitive Slave Law, and a resulting court case—*Ableman v. Booth.*

Jeffery, Julie Roy. *Abolitionists Remember: Antislavery Autobiographies & the Unfinished Work of Emancipation.* Chapel Hill, NC: University of North Carolina Press, 2008.

A documentary of the post–Civil War reminiscences of several abolitionists from Reconstruction through 1905 (and an additional memoir not published until 1996). Published during the Gilded Age, these egalitarian works were mostly not well received by the general reading public at that time.

Jones, Howard. *Mutiny on the* Amistad: *The Saga of a Slave Revolt and Its Impact on American Abolition, Law, and Diplomacy.* New York: Oxford University Press, 1987.

A scholarly account that is generally considered the standard work on the topic today.

Jordan, Ryan P. *Slavery and the Meetinghouse: The Quakers and the Abolitionist Dilemma, 1820–1865.* Bloomington, IN: University of Indiana Press, 2007.

A brief but scholarly book showing the complexity of thought among Quakers on slavery and abolitionism. Contrary to the popular oversimplification, they were no more uniform in their views than any other Christian group.

Katz, William Loren. *Breaking the Chains: African-American Slave Resistance.* New York: Aladdin Paperbacks, 1998 ed.

A brief, undocumented primer for students on the topic of slave revolts that also contains noteworthy illustrations.

Katz, William Loren, ed. *Thoughts on African Colonization.* New York: Arno Press, 1968.

A reprint of William Lloyd Garrison's definitive study designed to kill the colonization movement and the American Colonization Society in 1832. Contains an editorial introduction putting Garrison's book into historical perspective.

Klein, Martin A. *Historical Dictionary of Slavery and Abolition.* Lanham, MD: Scarecrow Press, 2002.

Very practical encyclopedia covering most of the major people and issues and events of the abolition movement.

Kolchin, Peter. *American Slavery, 1619–1877.* New York: Hill and Wang, 1993.

Regarded as one of the best brief, overarching surveys of the whole history of American slavery available. A good starting point for students to get introduced to the topic.

Irons, Charles F. *The Origins of Proslavery Christianity: White and Black Evangelicals in Colonial and Antebellum Virginia.* Chapel Hill, NC: University of North Carolina Press, 2008.

A scholarly book showing the pervasiveness of so-called and self-described evangelicalism among black and white Virginians in the 1850s. Proves that parts of the South were far more religious than is commonly thought on the eve of the Civil War.

Lader, Lawrence. *The Bold Brahmins: New England's War Against Slavery: 1832–1863.* New York: E.P. Dutton & Co., 1961.

A long, detailed account written for lay readers rather than scholars that focuses on the Boston elite's role in the movement.

Lerner, Gerda. *The Grimke Sisters from South Carolina: Pioneers for Women's Rights and Abolition.* New York: Schocken, 1983.

A long, thorough, definitive biography of the Grimkes.

Link, William A. *Roots of Secession: Slavery and Politics in Antebellum Virginia.* Chapel Hill, NC: University of North Carolina Press, 2003.

Focuses on issues and events in Virginia in the 1850s leading it to secede in 1861, such as the Fugitive Slave Act of 1850 and John Brown's Raid on Harpers Ferry.

Lumpkin, Katherine Du Pre. *The Emancipation of Angelina Grimke.* Chapel Hill, NC: University of North Carolina Press, 1974.

A thorough, scholarly, standard biography of Grimke.

Magdol, Edward. *Owen Lovejoy: Abolitionist in Congress.* New Brunswick, NJ: Rutgers University Press, 1967.

Long, scholarly biography that shows Lovejoy to be, similar to Joshua Giddings and John P. Hale, among others, one of the really important but mostly forgotten political figures of the abolition movement.

Marcus, Robert D., David Burner, and Anthony Marcus, eds. *America Firsthand: Volume One—Readings from Settlement to Reconstruction.* 7th ed. Boston: Bedford/St. Martin's, 2007.

A collection of primary documents, some of which help illuminate the abolition movement.

Martin, Christopher. *The* Amistad *Affair.* London: Abelard-Schuman, 1970.

A sparingly documented but otherwise fairly thorough version of the topic.

Mason, Marcia J. Heringa, ed. *Remember the Distance that Divides Us: The Family Letters of Philadelphia Quaker Abolitionist and Michigan Pioneer Elizabeth Margaret Chandler, 1830–1842.* East Lansing, MI: Michigan State University Press, 2004.

A long, scholarly collection of correspondence with an editorial introduction that places this marginal abolitionist in historical perspective.

McCarthy, Timothy Patrick and John Stauffer. *Prophets of Protest: Reconsidering the History of American Abolitionism.* New York: The New Press, 2006.

A collection of 15 essays by scholars in the field exploring the difficulty of researching and writing about slavery and abolition without making moral judgments on the topic.

McColley, Robert. *Slavery and Jeffersonian Virginia.* Urbana, IL: University of Illinois Press, 1964.

A good primer for learning about slavery and abolitionism in the founding generation and in the state that was the trendsetter among southern states in national politics. Particularly useful for studying the issue of manumission.

McFeely, William S. *Frederick Douglass.* New York: W.W. Norton, 1991.

A long, thorough biography using the popular new journalistic citation method rather than traditional footnotes or endnotes.

McKay, Ernest. *Henry Wilson, Practical Radical: A Portrait of a Politician.* Port Washington, NY: Kennikat Press, 1971.

The standard biography of one of the most important but largely forgotten figures in the abolition movement and who served as U.S. vice president in the 1870s.

McKitrick, Eric L., ed. *Slavery Defended: the Views of the Old South.* Englewood Cliffs, NJ: Prentice-Hall, 1963.

Editorial introduction followed by 17 primary source essays written by proslavery apologists such as John C. Calhoun and J. D. B. De Bow. Brief and readable and recommended for students and lay readers.

McKivigan, John R., ed. *Abolitionism and American Politics and Government.* New York: Garland, 1999.

Scholarly and long, as are most of McKivigan's books.

McKivigan, John R. and Mitchell Snay. *Religion and the Antebellum Debate over Slavery* Athens, GA: University of Georgia Press, 1998.

A long, scholarly collection of 12 essays exploring all different aspects of religious thought about slavery in the North and South among various denominations. Emphasizes the 1840s to 1860s time period.

McPherson, James M., ed. *An Appeal in Favor of that Class of Americans Called Africans.* New York: Arno Press, 1968.

A reprint of Lydia Maria Child's seminal abolitionist book published in 1836, which contains an editorial introduction putting Child and her work into historical perspective.

Mellon, James, ed. *Bullwhip Days: The Slaves Remember—An Oral History.* New York: Avon Books, 1988.

Slave narratives and topical vignettes taken from the WPA Collection of the 1930s.

Merrill, Walter M. *Against Wind and Tide: A Biography of William Lloyd Garrison.* Cambridge, MA: Harvard University Press, 1963.

A long, scholarly biography that covers more of Garrison's private life than some other biographies do while still documenting his abolitionist work thoroughly.

Merrill, Walter M. and Louis Ruchames, eds. *The Letters of William Lloyd Garrison.* Cambridge, MA: Belknap Press, 1971–1981.

A seven-volume set, with each volume containing at least 200 letters to or from Garrison.

Moore, Glover. *The Missouri Controversy, 1819–1821.* Lexington, KY: University Press of Kentucky, 1953.

The standard treatment of the topic.

Moore, Wilbert E. *American Negro Slavery and Abolition: A Sociological Study.* New York: The Third Press, 1971.

Mostly a broad survey of slavery and abolition but from a sociologist's perspective rather than a historian's, such that it is more analytical and less chronological than most narrative histories of the subject. Written at the time that cliometrics began to be a fad in historical writing.

Morgan, Edmund S. *American Slavery, American Freedom: The Ordeal of Colonial Virginia.* New York: W.W. Norton & Company, 1975.

The standard work on this topic for many years. Long and scholarly but covers only the first 70 years of the colonization of Virginia.

Nelson, Truman. *The Old Man: John Brown at Harper's Ferry.* New York: Holt, Rinehart, and Winston, 1973.

A well-written and argued book by a journalist rather than a historian. Contains excellent illustrations but lacks footnotes or endnotes; instead has a one-paragraph explanation of the sources used.

Niven, John, James P. McClure, Leigh Johnsen, et al., eds. *The Salmon P. Chase Papers.* Kent, OH: The Kent State University Press, 1993–1998.

Five-volume set containing journals and correspondence of one of the most important political abolitionists of the 1840s to 1860s.

Oates, Stephen B. *To Purge This Land with Blood: A Biography of John Brown,* 2nd ed. Amherst, MA: The University of Massachusetts Press, 1984.

Has been one of the standard treatments of this topic for many years. Scholarly but not esoteric, and thorough but not overly long.

Osagie, Iyunolu F. *The* Amistad *Revolt: Memory, Slavery and the Politics of Identity in the United States and Sierra Leone.* Athens, GA: University of Georgia Press, 2000.

A scholarly look at the *Amistad* story in modern American pop culture and historic memory. Also focuses on the modern African perspective on the story as seen from Sierra Leone, as well as on Hollywood's portrayals of the story.

Osofsky, Gilbert, ed. *Puttin' on Ole Massa.* New York: Harper & Row, 1969.

Contains valuable primary sources on slavery from the slaves' perspective.

Owens, William A. *Slave Mutiny: The Revolt on the Schooner Amistad*. New York: The John Day Company, 1953.

Not scholarly, documented history but rather a fictional "dramatic telling" of the story of the *Amistad* based on the rudimentary facts.

Parent, Anthony S., Jr. *Foul Means: The Formation of a Slave Society in Virginia, 1660–1740*. Chapel Hill, NC: University of North Carolina Press, 2003.

A detailed, scholarly account of the origins of slavery and the planter class in Virginia during the Colonial Era.

Pasternak, Martin B. *Rise Now and Fly to Arms: The Life of Henry Highland Garnet*. New York: Garland Publishing, 1995.

A brief but scholarly and sympathetic biography covering Garnet's whole life, ending with his death in Liberia in 1881.

Peterson, Merrill D. *John Brown: The Legend Revisited*. Charlottesville, VA: University of Virginia Press, 2002.

A brief reflection about Brown's image in the popular imagination by one of the preeminent scholars in American historical biography.

Quarles, Benjamin. *Black Abolitionists*. New York: Oxford University Press, 1969.

A scholarly but accessible account beginning with Paul Cuffe in the early 1800s to the outbreak of the Civil War written by one of the foremost early scholars of black history.

Quarles, Benjamin. *Lincoln and the Negro*. New York: Oxford University Press, 1962.

A scholarly, standard interpretation that shows Lincoln to be the Great Emancipator, not the great racist that some revisionists later portrayed him as. Does not use footnotes but has extensive list of sources cited at the end of each chapter.

Quarles, Benjamin, ed. *Narrative of the Life of Frederick Douglass, An American Slave, Written by Himself.* Cambridge, MA: The Belknap Press, 1967.

Contains an editorial introduction, chronology, map of the region of Maryland where Douglass lived in slavery, and the narrative itself.

Ratner, Lorman A. and Dwight L. Teeter, Jr. *Fanatics and Fire-eaters: Newspapers and the Coming of the Civil War.* Urbana, IL: University of Illinois Press, 2003.

Looks at six events from 1856 to 1861: the caning of Sumner, the Dred Scott case controversy, the Lecompton Constitution controversy, the raid on Harpers Ferry, the election of Lincoln, and the firing on Fort Sumter. Shows the role that radicals on both sides of the slavery debate played in banging the drums of war over these events.

Rawick, George P., ed. *The American Slave: A Composite Autobiography.* Westport, CT: Greenwood Press, 1969–1979.

Primary source. Multivolume set of slave narratives collected by the WPA in the 1930s. The definitive collection of its kind.

Reynolds, David S. *John Brown, Abolitionist: The Man Who Killed Slavery, Sparked the Civil War, and Seeded Civil Rights.* New York: Alfred A. Knopf, 2005.

A laudatory account of Brown's importance in American history, as the title suggests. Long and scholarly. Uses the new journalistic style of endnotes.

Richardson, H. Edward. *Cassius Marcellus Clay: Firebrand of Freedom.* Lexington, KY: University Press of Kentucky, 1976.

A standard biography of one of the most important southern abolitionists. Contains a thorough bibliography but does not contain footnotes or endnotes. Emphasizes the role of William Lloyd Garrison in converting Clay to abolitionism.

Robertson, Stacey M. *Parker Pillsbury: Radical Abolitionist, Male Feminist.* Ithaca, NY: Cornell University Press, 2000.

A scholarly biography of an important but marginal abolitionist who is most remembered for writing *Acts of the Anti-Slavery Apostles* (1883), an important first-hand account of the movement.

Robinson, Donald. *Slavery in the Structure of American Politics, 1765–1820.* New York: W.W. Norton & Company, 1979 ed.

A scholarly account of the growth of slavery in the United States and the incorporation of this growth into the decision making of the U.S. government up to the time of the Missouri Controversy.

Rodriguez, Junius, ed. *Encyclopedia of Emancipation and Abolition in the Transatlantic World.* Armonk, NY: Sharpe Reference, 2007.

The definitive encyclopedia of the abolition movement. Highly recommended as a starting point for students researching the topic.

Rosengarten, Theodore, ed. *Tombee: Portrait of a Planter.* New York: Quill, 1986.

Primary source. The published *Journal of Thomas B. Chaplin* of South Carolina. Shows slavery from a white planter's perspective.

Rozwenc, Edwin C., ed. *Slavery as a Cause of the Civil War.* Boston: D.C. Heath and Company, 1949.

A brief and somewhat outdated but still valuable collection of essays showing the evolution of the historiography of the question of whether slavery was really the cause of the war or merely one of several causes.

Rozwenc, Edwin C. and Wayne A. Frederick. *Slavery and the Breakdown of the American Consensus.* Boston: D.C. Heath and Company, 1964.

A brief sociological study positing that there was a consensus in America before the Civil War in which antislavery and proslavery people basically agreed to tolerate each other for the sake of national harmony. The advent of the Republican Party broke the consensus. Contains primary and historiographical interpretations.

Schwartz, Philip J. *Migrants against Slavery: Virginians and the Nation.* Charlottesville, VA: University of Virginia Press, 2001.

A brief but scholarly documentary of the history of freed slaves leaving Virginia for free states or foreign countries.

Scott, John A., ed. *Journal of a Residence on a Georgian Plantation in 1838–1839*. 1863; reprint. Athens: University of Georgia Press, 1984.

Primary source. Journal of Fannie Kemble, which abolitionists used to bolster their case against slavery.

Sernett, Milton C. *Harriet Tubman: Myth, Memory, and History*. Durham, NC: Duke University Press, 2007.

A scholarly analysis of the legend of Tubman. Tells virtually everything there is to know about her but is not a standard biography. Contains excellent illustrations.

Sewell, Richard H. *John P. Hale and the Politics of Abolition*. Cambridge, MA: Harvard University Press, 1965.

Standard biography of a man who had been a U.S. senator from New Hampshire and was nominated for the presidency on the Liberty League ticket in 1848 but thereafter became one of the largely forgotten figures in the abolition movement.

Smith, Elbert B. *The Death of Slavery: The United States, 1837–1865*. Chicago: University of Chicago Press, 1967.

An excellent, brief, scholarly political history of how and why slavery was abolished. Contains a timeline and a bibliography but does not offer footnotes or endnotes.

Smith, John David. *An Old Creed for the New South: Proslavery Ideology and Historiography, 1865–1918*. Athens, GA: University of Georgia Press, 1991.

A scholarly look at how proslavery (and consequently antiegalitarian, paternalistic, racist thought) carried over from the Old South to all of the United States in the Jim Crow era, being perpetuated and reinforced by history books written from that point of view.

Soderlund, Jean R. *Quakers and Slavery: A Divided Spirit*. Princeton, NJ: Princeton University Press, 1985.

A sociological or cliometric study of the Quakers in the Delaware Valley in the 1700s in terms of slave ownership or opposition to slavery.

Stampp, Kenneth. *The Peculiar Institution: Slavery in the Ante-Bellum South.* 1956; reprint. New York: Vintage Books, 1964.

The standard treatment of the topic for many years but superseded by Peter Kolchin's book in recent years.

Sterling, Dorothy. *Ahead of Her Time: Abby Kelley and the Politics of Anti-Slavery.* New York: W.W. Norton, 1991.

A long, scholarly, definitive biography of one of the most important female abolitionists. Contains superb illustrations of leading figures of the movement.

Stewart, James Brewer. *Holy Warriors: The Abolitionists and American Slavery.* New York: Hill and Wang, 1996.

A good, brief treatment that focuses on the religious motivations of most abolitionists.

Stewart, James Brewer. *Joshua R. Giddings and the Tactics of Radical Politics.* Cleveland, OH: The Press of Case Western Reserve University, 1970.

Standard, sympathetic biography showing Giddings to have been more worthy of being lionized as a hero of the abolition movement than the nonpolitical William Lloyd Garrison because he actually worked in the U.S. government to achieve change rather than standing at a distance calling for disunion.

Still, William. *The Underground Railroad.* 1872; reprint. Chicago: Johnson, 1970.

First-person eyewitness account written by the man who first began compiling information on the Underground Railroad.

Strong, Douglas M. *Perfectionist Politics: Abolitionism and the Religious Tensions of American Democracy.* Syracuse, NY: Syracuse University Press, 2000.

A short but scholarly book focusing on New York's evangelical movement in the 1830s and the role it played in the abolition movement as a whole.

Tappan, Lewis. *The Life of Arthur Tappan*. New York: Hurd & Houghton, 1871.

Long primary or first-hand biography of the main bankroller of the abolition movement, written in glowing memoriam.

Thomas, Benjamin P. *Theodore Weld: Crusader for Freedom*. New Brunswick, NJ: Rutgers University Press, 1950.

The first published full-length biography of Weld. Written in scholarly but accessible narrative form.

Thomas, John L., ed. *Slavery Attacked: The Abolitionist Crusade*. Englewood Cliffs, NJ: Prentice Hall, 1965.

Primary documents. Valuable source with excellent editorial notes.

Toledo, Gregory. *The Hanging of Old Brown: A Story of Slaves, Statesmen, and Redemption*. Westport, CT: Praeger, 2002.

Starts with two chapters surveying the history of slavery and abolitionism in America before the emergence of Brown as a national figure followed by a standard biography of Brown. Thorough and scholarly. Highly recommended.

Trefousse, H. L. *Benjamin Franklin Wade: Radical Republican from Ohio*. New York: Twayne Publishers, 1963.

The standard biography of the abolitionist senator who went on to play a major role in the impeachment of Andrew Johnson and came within one vote of becoming U.S. president himself.

Vorenberg, Michael. *Final Freedom: The Civil War, the Abolition of Slavery, and the Thirteenth Amendment*. Cambridge, UK: Cambridge University Press, 2001.

A scholarly look at various constitutional issues pertaining to slavery. Explores the various interpretations and applications of the 13th Amendment as viewed from the 1860s to 1870s.

Walker, Peter F. *Moral Choices: Memory, Desire, and Imagination in Nineteenth-Century American Abolition.* Baton Rouge, LA: Louisiana State University Press, 1978.

A psychohistory that looks mostly at obscure or marginal abolitionists such as Moncure Conway, Jane Gray Swisshelm, Henry Wrigth, Salmon Chase, and Thomas Cooley but also contains a section on Frederick Douglass.

Walther, Eric H. *The Fire-Eaters.* Baton Rouge, LA: Louisiana State University Press, 1992.

Scholarly account of nine of the leading Fire-Eaters. Defines the term, identifies who was and was not a Fire-Eater, and portrays them as tragic figures in a lost cause but is not sympathetic to them.

Weld, Theodore D. *Slavery As It Is: Testimony of a Thousand Witnesses.* 1839; reprint. New York: Arno Press, 1969.

One of the classic, indispensible primary sources from the abolition movement.

Wieck, Carl F. *Lincoln's Quest for Equality: The Road to Gettysburg.* DeKalb, IL: Northern Illinois University Press, 2002.

A brief but scholarly book showing that the Boston Transcendentalist Theodore Parker was the driving force behind Lincoln's conversion to a racial egalitarian during the war.

Wilbanks, Charles, ed. *Walking by Faith: The Diary of Angelina Grimke.* Columbia, SC: University of South Carolina Press, 2003.

Contains a brief but thorough editorial introduction followed by the complete 337-page diary, which is dated 1828 to 1835.

Wilentz, Sean, ed. *Major Problems in the Early Republic, 1787–1848: Documents and Essays.* Lexington, MA: D.C. Heath and Company, 1992.

Primary sources along with secondary articles and editorials.

Willey, Austin. *The History of the Anti-Slavery Cause in State and Nation.* 1860; reprint. New York: Negro Universities Press 1969.

First-hand account by a Calvinist preacher from Maine, heavily focusing on Maine's role in the movement.

Williams, Robert C. *Horace Greeley: Champion of American Freedom*. New York: New York University Press, 2006.

Scholarly biography calling Greeley an antislavery man rather than an abolitionist and explains the difference.

Wilson, Henry. *History of the Rise and Fall of the Slave Power in America*. Boston: J. R. Osgood and Company, 1872.

Primary, first generation, and eyewitness account by an abolitionist who later became vice president of the United States. Three volumes.

Wilson, Jos. T. *Emancipation: Its Course and Progress, from 1481 to 1875*. 1882; reprint. New York: Negro Universities Press, 1969.

Gives a brief but important overview of the whole history of world slavery as far as this author understood it in the 1880s. A contemporary if not primary source written from an abolitionist's point of view.

Windley, Lathan A. *Runaway Slave Advertisements: A Documentary History from the 1730s to 1790*. Westport, CT: Greenwood Press, 1983.

Primary source material taken mostly from newspaper advertisements in Virginia, North Carolina, Maryland, South Carolina, and Georgia. Packaged in four separate volumes, the advertisements are in type print and are translated verbatim. Covers the six decades between the founding of Georgia and the passing of the first Fugitive Slave Law.

Wish, Harvey. *George Fitzhugh: Propagandist of the Old South*. Gloucester, MA: Peter Smith, 1962.

A long, scholarly biography that reveals the complexity of Fitzhugh's thought. Shows that he was not a bigoted racist so much as an intellectual sociologist–philosopher who theorized grand, sweeping ideas about individual freedom vis-à-vis societal order and good government.

Wolf, Eva Sheppard. *Race and Liberty in the New Nation: Emancipation in Virginia from the Revolution to Nat Turner's Rebellion.* Baton Rouge, LA: Louisiana State University Press, 2006.

Expands on the work of Robert McColley, looking at the debate over emancipation in the Early Republic before the Nat Turner rebellion goaded Virginia into becoming radically proslavery.

Yee, Shirley. *Black Women Abolitionists: A Study in Activism, 1828–1860.* Knoxville, TN: University of Tennessee Press, 1994.

A brief but scholarly introduction to the topic. Recommended as a primer for students interested in the intersection of women's history and black abolitionism.

Young, Jeffrey Robert. *Proslavery and Sectional Thought in the Early South, 1740–1829: An Anthology.* Columbia, SC: University of South Carolina Press, 2006.

A scholarly collection of 13 chapters, each of which deals with an individual or location—mostly obscure rather than famous—beginning with the founding of the Georgia colony in the 1730s to the start of the abolition movement in the 1830s.

Zilversmit, Arthur. *Lincoln on Black and White: A Documentary History.* Malabar, FL: Robert E. Kreiger Publishing Company, 1983.

Perhaps the definitive examination of Lincoln's complex, nuanced, and seemingly contradictory racial views. Excellent editorial introduction showing the historiography of the topic followed by 81 primary documents, mostly of Lincoln's speeches and letters.

Zilversmit, Arthur, *The First Emancipation: The Abolition of Slavery in the North.* Chicago: The University of Chicago Press, 1967.

A scholarly work tracing abolitionism's history in each northern state but also painting an overall portrait of slavery in the North as contrasted with the stereotypes of the South.

Websites

DigitalHistory. http://www.digitalhistory.uh.edu/other_documents/other_documents.cfm.

Contains some key primary source documents on slavery and abolition.

Documenting the American South. http://docsouth.unc.edu.

Particularly useful for its vast collection of slave narratives. Makes having hard copies of most first-hand accounts of slavery and abolitionism unnecessary.

Samuel J. May Anti-Slavery Collection. http://digital. library.cornell .edu/m/mayantislavery.

An invaluable assortment of primary documents covering virtually the whole history of the abolition movement, including newspaper articles, sermons, and pamphlets from both the United States and Great Britain.

Index

About the Author

T. ADAMS UPCHURCH is Associate Professor of History at East Georgia College. He is the author of *Legislating Racism: The Billion Dollar Congress and the Birth of Jim Crow* (University Press of Kentucky, 2004); *A White Minority in Post-Civil Rights Mississippi* (Hamilton, 2005); *Race Relations in the United States, 1960–1980* (Greenwood, 2007); *Historical Dictionary of the Gilded Age* (Scarecrow, 2009); and *Christian Nation? The United States in Popular Perception and Historical Reality* (Praeger, 2010).